When is nationalism ethically acceptable?

In beautifully simple language, Gregory Baum discusses the writings of four men whose nationalism was shaped by their religion and their time: Martin Buber's speeches on Zionism before the creation of Israel; Mahatma Gandhi's influential incitement to peaceful resistance against British imperialism; Paul Tillich's book on socialism and nationalism which was banned by the Nazis; and Jacques Grand'Maison's defence of Quebecois nationalism in the wake of the province's Quiet Revolution.

Baum also examines nationalism in a world dominated by transnational corporations and economic globalization: for example, how does Scottish nationalism fit within the European Union, and how can the Church of Scotland contribute to this secular movement? Finally, Baum turns to Quebec and its tension between ethnic and civil nationalism. As a province with a homogenous and distinctive culture that is different from that of the country surrounding it, how can Quebec guarantee its own survival in an ethically acceptable way?

This quiet masterpiece of clear thinking and humane reasoning illuminates the uses and misdirections of one of the most powerful forces in politics and society.

GREGORY BAUM is professor emeritus of theological ethics and sociology of religion, McGill University. He has participated in the CBC Massey Lecture Series and is an officer of the Order of Canada.

Nationalism, Religion, and Ethics

Gregory Baum

McGill-Queen's University Press
Montreal & Kingston · London · Ithaca

© McGill-Queen's University Press 2001
ISBN 0-7735-2242-5 (cloth)
ISBN 0-7735-2278-6 (paperback)

Legal deposit third quarter 2001
Bibliothèque nationale du Québec

Printed in Canada on acid-free paper

McGill-Queen's University Press acknowledges
the financial support of the Government of Canada
through the Book Publishing Industry Development
Program (BPIDP) for its activities.
It also acknowledges the support of the Canada
Couceil for the Arts for its publishing program.

**National Library of Canada Cataloguing
in Publication Data**

Baum, Gregory, 1923–
Nationalism, religion, and ethics
Includes bibliographical references and index.
ISBN 0-7735-22-42-5 (bound) –
ISBN 0-7735-2278-6 (pbk.)
1. Nationalism – Moral and ethical aspects.
2. Nationalism – Religious aspects. 3. Buber, Martin,
1878–1965 – Views on nationalism. 4. Gandhi,
Mahatma, 1869–1948. 5. Tillich, Paul, 1886–1965 –
Views on nationalism. 6. Grand'Maison, Jacques,
1931– – Views on nationalism. 7. Nationalism –
Moral and ethical aspects – Quebec (Province).
8. Nationalism – Quebec (Province) – Religious
aspects. 1. Title.
JC311.B38 2001   172   C2001-900262-9

Typeset in Adobe Garamond 10.5/13
by Caractéra inc., Quebec City

Available in French as
Le nationalisme: perspectives éthiques et religieuses,
published by Éditions Bellarmin.

To my friends at
le Centre justice et foi

Contents

Nationalism, Religion, and Ethics

Ethics and the Polymorphous Phenomenon of Nationalism

Nationalism is a confusing historical phenomenon. Those of my generation remember the aggressive, murderous nationalism of Nazi Germany, and some people continue to think of nationalism as a political movement close to fascism. We are presently appalled by the outbreak of militant nationalism in several regions of Eastern Europe that previously were ruled by a communist government. At the same time, history books usually present the American Revolution as a nationalist, anti-colonial movement that deserves admiration. Similarly, many people have had a great deal of sympathy for the anti-imperialist nationalism of the former colonies in Asia and Africa struggling to become independent states; their political efforts received international approval in the 1966 Covenant of the United Nations which recognized the right of nations or peoples to cultural and political self-determination.[1] We are not used to relating these various phenomena to one another. Friends of mine, academics among them, who strongly disapprove of nationalism, enjoyed the great American film on the life of Gandhi, which glorified Indian nationalism in its struggle against the British empire for independent statehood. Because nationalism is such a polymorphous phenomenon, we are often confused by it and react to it without careful political analysis. Since the nationalist movement in Quebec and the demand for self-government on the part of the Native peoples are for many Canadians disturbing developments, there is special need for critical thinking. What interests me in this book are ethical reflections on nationalism.

While it is difficult to judge a nationalist movement looking at it from the outside, it is, of course, also difficult to evaluate it from the inside. How, for instance, did Christians living in North America at the time of the American Revolution evaluate the political struggle to define a group of British colonies as a new nation, vindicate its right to political self-determination, and repudiate the jurisdiction of the British Crown? Christians were deeply divided by the Revolution, and they defended their respective positions with ethical arguments drawn from the Scriptures. The historian Mark Noll distinguishes four different camps within the Christian community.[2] The nationalists, or patriots as they were then called, invoked the biblical story of the Exodus and likened King George to King Pharaoh who would not let the people go; their preachers adopted very passionate tones in support of the Revolution. A second group supported the Revolution but held that it was biblically justified only if it was accompanied by the conversion of the new nation to greater obedience to God's commandments. Some preachers even suggested that if Americans claimed the ethical right to assume political sovereignty, they should be ready to grant freedom to their black slaves. A third group opposed the Revolution. Relying on the biblical texts that demand obedience to legitimate authority, in particular Romans 13:1–5, they remained faithful to the British Crown. Canadians are well aware of this latter group because many of the Empire Loyalists, as they were called, moved to the northern British colonies that were to become the dominion of Canada. A fourth group of Christians, mainly Quakers and Mennonites, opposed the Revolution because as pacifists they repudiated the use of violence. This American Christian experience shows how difficult it is for a people to evaluate a nationalist movement organized in their own midst.

AN ETHICS FOR NATIONALISM ABSENT IN THE CATHOLIC TRADITION

There exists little systematic theological or ethical reflection on the polymorphous phenomenon of nationalism. What impressed me as a Catholic theologian was that Catholic Social Teaching, which constitutes an impressive body of literature and provides a rich source of social and economic ethics, offers no systematic treatment of nationalism. In the papal encyclicals dealing with social issues nationalism is hardly ever mentioned.[3] While Catholic Social Teaching has offered original ideas in response to the economic crises in Western society, it has almost nothing to say in response to the nationalist crises in the world. Nor did the evolution of the Church's social teaching during and after Vatican Council II produce serious ethical reflection on the topic of nationalism. Even the recent, otherwise excellent *New Dictionary of Catholic Social Thought*,[4] published in the United States, carries no article on nationalism.

What is the reason for this lacuna? One reason is the fact that in the nineteenth century the Catholic Church had strongly repudiated nationalism. At that time, the papacy was allied with the feudal-aristocratic order and the conservative sector of European society, and it vigorously opposed the new ideas of popular sovereignty, the liberal state, the concept of citizenship, the separation of church and state, and the concession of civil liberties. The Syllabus of Errors of 1866 remains an important witness to this phase of the Church's history. The papacy looked upon nationalism as a political and cultural force that fostered secularization and undermined even further the unity of Europe's Christian civilization.

But this was not all. Nationalism posed a particular threat to the papacy. In the Middle Ages the popes had acquired secular rule over certain regions on Italian and French soil, the so-called states of the Church. In 1791 the French republic confiscated the papal state on French soil, and half a century later, Italian nationalism, wrestling against the remnants of the feudal order, intended to abolish the papal state on Italian soil. When the papal army was defeated in 1861, Pius IX lost his entire territory with the exception of the city of Rome. In 1870, Rome itself was lost and the Pope withdrew into the Vatican. He regarded himself a political prisoner, refused to recognize the legitimacy of the new Italian state, and forbade Catholics to vote and participate in the country's political life. These experiences reinforced papal opposition to nationalism.

At the same time, by a curious paradox, a new kind of nationalism that had a special appeal for Catholics was emerging in several countries. When the nation-state created by the bourgeoisie fostered a secular, republican culture, which tolerated atheism and religious pluralism and favoured the capitalist virtues of individualism, materialism, and personal ambition, conservatives attached to the traditional virtues became critical of modernity and material progress, and advocated the return of people to the ethos of community and to their religious and ethnic roots. This movement existed in different forms.

One form consisted of an attachment to the *ancien régime*. In France we find a conservative movement, strongly supported by Catholics, that opposed the rational, universalist values of the republic, cultivated the memory of past national glories, and advocated the restoration of the monarchy. Here nationalism ceased to signify the struggle for popular sovereignty, equal citizenship, and the formation of the modern state; it became instead a conservative movement within the modern state, opposed to equality and democracy and supporting the social hierarchy inherited from the past. This nationalism disapproved of the civil liberties: it stood against freedom of speech and religious pluralism. Since in the modern state Jews had become citizens on an equal footing and come to play an important role in science, the arts, and politics, they were looked upon by conservatives as agents and symbols of liberalism and consequently hated. In France the new nationalism was antisemitic, and it had strong Catholic support. A typical example is the vehemence with which the Catholic clergy and the Catholic press demanded the condemnation of Captain Dreyfus, even when the evidence against him fell apart.

Yet at the same time in France there existed another form of nationalism, one that was critical of the *ancien régime*, defended civil liberties, expressed solidarity with the poor, and had a reformist thrust. Charles Péguy, the remarkable thinker and poet, long dedicated to the virtues of the republic, was one of the most eloquent defenders of the innocent Dreyfus. Péguy regarded antisemitism as a betrayal of the genius of France. Inspired by the vision of a just and humane society transcending the differences created by wealth and inherited privilege, he became critical of the dominant republican discourse because it expressed contempt for the culture and religious sentiment of the ordinary people. Severed from their roots, Péguy argued, people lose their sense of social solidarity and become exclusively concerned with their own advancement. Péguy became a nationalist, yet without abandoning his egalitarian ideal. Once a passionate secularist, he now became a Catholic. Faith became the important dimension of his life. At this time he wrote his most moving poetry. Yet he refused to attend Mass, the Church's public worship. Why? Since he had always been in solidarity with the marginalized and excluded, he did not want to join the Catholic upright estab-lishment that divided humanity into "us," the superior, and "them," the inferior.[5] Martin Buber, as we shall see, referred to Péguy's nationalism with admiration.

No general Catholic theory dealing with the ethics of nation-alist movements existed at that time. There was only confu-sion. The papacy did not endorse the conservative nationalism supported by French Catholics, nor did it support the anti-imperialist nationalism of the Irish demanding home rule from Great Britain. To this day, there is no Catholic theory to offer guidance to nationalist movements in Catholic coun-tries such as Poland or Croatia. A recent report on an ecu-menical meeting held in Belgrade involving Christian leaders from various parts of the former Yugoslavia revealed an almost total absence of theological and ethical reflection.[6] The par-ticipants did not, on the whole, see themselves as heirs of a tradition that brought them wisdom in regard to nationalism.

RECENT REFLECTIONS ON NATIONALISM BY REGIONAL CHURCHES

To my knowledge the only Catholic bishops who have offered critical reflections on nationalism and provided their people with ethical guidelines are the bishops of Quebec. Quebecers see themselves as a nation within the Canadian Confederation and are presently wrestling with the question of whether they can thrive as a people within Canada or whether they should opt for political sovereignty. From the beginning, they say, the Canadian Confederation of 1867 produced an unequal union, putting French Canada at a cultural, economic, and political disadvantage. They add to this that today Canada no longer sees itself as a union between two national communities. English-speaking Canadians prefer to define their country as a Con-federation of ten equal provinces. In this situation Quebecers ask themselves whether their provincial government has the power necessary to promote the interests of the small French-speaking nation and protect it from gradual assimilation and eventual disappearance.

Before the referendum on sovereignty of 1980 (which was lost), the Catholic bishops published two pastoral letters offering critical ethical reflections on nationalism.[7] Theirs was a remarkable achievement.[8]

From the outset the bishops recognize Quebecers as a people. In a reference to the 1966 Covenant of the United Nations, they say that the conscience of humanity has come to recognize the right of a people to political self-determination. This right, they argue, applies to "le peuple québécois." But who are these Quebec people? As a group rooted in the French colonial foundation over three hundred years ago and shaped by subsequent historical experiences, it can no longer be defined solely in ethnic terms. "Le peuple québécois," the bishops write, have over the years been open to people of other origins and the term now embraces all people living on its territory, including the First Nations with their special rights, the English community with its historic institutions, and the more recent immigrants and their descendants. Today, allow me to add, ethnically French Quebecers make up eighty per cent of the population of Quebec.

The bishops declare that it is not their task and responsibility to tell Catholics how to vote: voters must make up their own minds as to how they see their nation's future, within Canada or beyond Canada. They do, however, declare a responsibility to formulate ethical guidelines for political action. The quest for national sovereignty, they continue, is ethical only i) if it aims at creating a more just and more open society, ii) if it respects the human rights of minorities, and iii) if it anticipates cooperating and living in peace with other nations. The bishops add a fourth point, that Catholics must not use "theological" arguments to defend their political option: they may say neither that the oppression of Quebec within Canada is such that God calls Christians to vote for sovereignty, nor that Canadian unity is blessed by God and hence to vote against it is a grave sin. The bishops warn here against giving the nation a sacred or religious nimbus. The nation may not be regarded as the highest good.

I wish to call the guidelines of the Quebec bishops "the fourfold ethical proviso" of nationalism. From what sources did the bishops of Quebec draw their critical reflections? They were undoubtedly familiar with the work of Quebec theologian Jacques Grand'Maison, whose *Nationalisme et religion* was published in 1970. They probably also consulted him personally. We shall study Grand'Maison's thought in chapter 5 of this book.

There are other examples in recent history of Churches, Catholic and Protestant, that have produced theological and ethical reflections on national identity and nationalism in their own historical context, and research on this topic remains to be done. I was greatly impressed by the official position adopted by the Protestant Church in East Germany, prior to the reunification of Germany in 1991.[9] After the division of Germany into two different countries, as punishment for unleashing an aggressive war and humiliating the conquered peoples, many Germans in the Eastern republic, especially Christians, remained unreconciled to the fact that they now lived under a communist government. They stayed sentimentally attached to the formerly united Germany, envied the freedom and the capitalist market enjoyed in the western republic, and hoped that East Germany was a dark cloud that would soon disappear. After about a decade the Protestant Church decided that this was not an appropriate Christian attitude, for two reasons. First, the Germans, and especially the Christians among them, should in humility accept the division of Germany as a just punishment for the inhuman crimes committed by Germans in the name of their country; they should also appreciate that this division now protected the peace of Europe. Second, Christian faith calls believers to assume responsibility for the society in which they live. The Church argued that Christians must embrace their nation as it is and act within it to make it a more just society. Since in the atmosphere of the Cold War the western nations, including West Germany, refused to recognize East Germany as a nation, the Church decided to defend the nationhood of its country and recommend – from their place at the World Council of Churches – that the newly formed nation receive international recognition. In this context the Church adopted a nationalist position. At the same time, the Church used the margin of freedom it had acquired in East Germany to support the peace movement, criticize the public rhetoric demonizing the West, oppose the emergence of a new militarism, defend the critics of the government when they were arrested, and give witness to what it called "the unbridgeable gulf" between Christian faith and the official Marxism.

Many voices in today's Germany, reunited since 1991, claim – in my opinion, without justification – that in defending the national identity of East Germany and adopting a reformist stance within it, the Protestant Church collaborated with a totalitarian regime. This accusation reflects a particular ideological agenda. The only "mistake" the Protestant bishops made was that they did not foresee the collapse of communism; very few observers did. In his encyclical *Sollicitudo rei socialis* of 30 December 1987, Pope John Paul II still assumed that communism was here to stay and that it was in principle reformable.[10]

Another example of a Church willing to wrestle with the topic of nationalism from an ethical perspective is the Church of Scotland, belonging to the Presbyterian or Reformed tradition. When in 1707 Scotland joined England in the creation of a single political realm, Great Britain, with its government located in London, the Church of Scotland became the principal institution that protected the identity of the Scottish nation. The Church embraced the nation, defined its culture, and formulated its vision of the future. One is reminded of the somewhat parallel situation of the Quebec Church after the British conquest. While in the nineteenth and the first part of the twentieth century Scotland became a modern, industrial society, its population remained on the whole loyal to the Church, recognizing it as the symbol of their national identity. During World War II the Church of Scotland endorsed, on ethical grounds, the ideals of social democracy, supported equally at that time by the Church of England, ideals which were eventually put into practice by the Labour government. At that time the statements of the Church of Scotland had a unionist rather than a nationalist ring.

Since then the historical situation of Scotland and its Church has changed dramatically. First, Scotland is no longer a Christian society. Because of sweeping secularization, the Church has come to represent a small minority within the nation. Second, the arrival of the Thatcher government, the attack on social democratic ideals, the globalization of the economy, the death of old industries like ship-building, the discovery of oil, and the movement toward the European Union have forced the Scots to rethink their social situation and their role in the world. Many of them now support a nationalist movement standing for social democracy against neo-conservatism, for national identity against global techno-culture, and for greater self-government against the centralizing power of Westminster. In this situation, the Church has rethought its own pastoral responsibility. Even if it is now a minority, the Church continues to see itself as a servant of the Scottish nation. The so-called "Church and Nation Committee," responsible for formulating the Church's social policy, recognizes the need to think and act ecumenically in cooperation with Catholics and Protestants of other traditions. The same committee now offers ethical considerations that support the new nationalism with its emphasis on social justice, cultural identity, and national self-determination, all the while remembering the evil deeds committed in the name of nationalism.[11]

THE IDEA OF THE PRESENT BOOK

The stories told in these pages illustrate the pluriform nature of nationalism as well as the scarcity of Christian ethical reflection on it. Because of this scarcity I have decided to study thinkers, and specifically religious thinkers, who offer norms or criteria distinguishing between ethically acceptable and ethically unacceptable forms of nationalism. Nationalist movements have been amply studied by historians and political scientists,[12] and some of these studies consider the problematic role played by religion in these movements. Yet very few authors, to my knowledge, have approached nationalism from an ethical perspective.

In this book I examine the ethical reflections on nationalism by Martin Buber, the Jewish religious philosopher; Mahatma Gandhi, the Hindu sage; Paul Tillich, the Protestant theologian; and Jacques Grand'Maison, the Catholic thinker mentioned above. Since these authors have produced an important corpus of books, articles, and speeches, I have limited my study to documents that deal specifically with the issue of nationalism. For Buber, I have focused on three speeches, *Reden über das Judentum*, given before World War I, and an address to the Zionist Congress of 1921; for Gandhi, I have examined his pamphlet *Hind Swaraj*, written in 1909, and his controversy on nationalism with the Indian poet Tagore after World War I; for Tillich, I have studied a major book of his, *Die sozialistische Entscheidung*, published in January 1933, a few weeks before Hitler came to power in Germany; and for Grand'Maison, I have analysed his two-volume work, *Nationalisme et religion*, published in 1970.

CANADIAN NATIONALISM

After long reflection I have decided not to include in this study the Canadian social philosopher George Grant, whose celebrated book, *Lament for a Nation*, published in 1965,[13] represents a form of Canadian nationalism. Canadian nationalism has been a political and cultural policy debated by politicians, intellectuals, and artists, yet it has never been a strong popular movement. At the foundation of Canada in 1867 the Conservative government under Sir John A. Macdonald adopted the so-called National Economic Policy offering tariff protection for the growing Canadian industries. In subsequent decades the continual debate in parliament was between the "nationalists" who believed Canadian development must be protected against American take-over and the "continentalists" who favoured free trade and argued that the Canadian development would benefit from integration into the American economy. This debate has never disappeared from Canadian political life.[14]

When, after World War II, Canada's political, economic, and cultural ties to Great Britain were gradually loosened, American power and influence were seen by many as a major threat to Canadian sovereignty and identity. The Massay Royal Commission of 1951 on the arts, letters, and sciences warned of the invasion of American culture; the Gordon Royal Commission of 1958 on Canada's economic prospects warned of American economic take-over and recommended limiting foreign ownership of public media; and the Watkin Task Force of 1968 on foreign ownership and the structure of Canadian industry drew an even more serious picture of a Canadian economy controlled by American interests. Yet the influence these appointed commissions had on the government was minimal. In 1970 the economist Kari Levitt published her book *Silent Surrender*,[15] which documented the Canadian unwillingness to resist American domination of their industries. In the seventies a group of politicians and intellectuals formed the "Committee for an Independent Canada"[16] which sought to influence public opinion and persuade the government to adopt economic and cultural policies to protect Canada's sovereignty and identity. These efforts were supported by Canada's social democratic party, the New Democrats. A few protective measures were indeed taken by government, but they did not last very long. On the whole, it must be admitted, Canadians paid little attention to these nationalist concerns. Were they gradually becoming Americans?

George Grant was the somewhat gloomy philosopher of Canadian nationalism. He located himself in a philosophical and social scientific tradition that was critical of modernity, or to be precise, the domination of techno-scientific reason. We have already described this current in connection with Charles Péguy, and we shall come back to it throughout this book. Some people encountered this critique in Heidegger or other existentialist philosophers, while others took it from critical sociologists, of whom Max Weber is the famous representative. Grant acknowledged his link to Heidegger. Technological progress, he argued, has become the new religion. Scientific rationalism severs people from their cultural and religious roots and undermines people's trust in ethical reasoning. The only value left is utility.

In *Lament for a Nation*, Grant argues that Canada had been a country rooted in tradition, British and French, respectful of justice, order, and right reason, and guided by a Christian humanist vision of society. This country, Grant continues, is about to disappear: it has been invaded by American-sponsored techno-culture, cut from its roots and deprived of its ethical values. Canadians have not resisted. Even the small efforts made by government – Grant is here thinking of Prime Minister Diefenbaker's nationalist policy – have not been supported by the Canadian people. The book laments in a moving and dignified manner the loss of a great national tradition of community spirit, moral sanity, and modest material expectations. Yet the impact of this gloomy book was the opposite of gloom. It inspired many intellectuals, artists, and politically engaged Canadians to take up the cause of Canada in their work. The Protestant theologian Douglas Hall gratefully acknowledged George Grant's influence on his thought and attitudes.[17]

Canadian nationalists were divided over their reaction to the new Quebec nationalism of the sixties. Some looked upon Quebec nationalism with admiration and wanted English Canada to imitate Quebec's bold cultural self-affirmation, while others were hostile, seeing it as a threat to Canadian unity.

The reason then why I decided not to examine George Grant's anti-imperialist Canadian nationalism in this book is that Canadian nationalism has never become a popular or mass-based movement; for this reason it may not be regarded as a parallel development to Quebec nationalism. Treating these two historical phenomena side by side would, in my opinion, create confusion.

*

Finally I must raise the question whether the ideas about nationalism worked out in the past retain any validity in the age into which we are now moving. What is the future of the nation-state? Is massive immigration changing the human topology on all continents? What reactions will there be against the universal spread of market-driven techno-culture and the ever-growing gap between rich and poor? In a recent article, Kari Levitt wonders whether the political concepts that helped us interpret historical developments in the industrial age are still useful for interpreting the political currents and social upheavals of the present.[18] I shall return to some of these questions at the end of this book.

2

Martin Buber's Ethic
of Nationalism

Martin Buber (1878–1965), the renowned Jewish religious philosopher, has been influential among Jews and Christians alike.
He is famous for uncovering the dialogical structure of human
existence and for proposing a humanistic interpretation of biblical religion. My focus on Buber here is limited to his idea of
nationalism and the ethical norms he prescribed for it. This
topic has been studied in a number of learned works on Buber's
social and political ideas.[1] It has been argued that his understanding of nationalism underwent an evolution from his early
proposals made before World War I to the later proposals
offered by him after that war. Both of his presentations deal
with the ethical question, even if from slightly different perspectives. In this chapter we look first at the early texts, Buber's three
speeches on Judaism given between 1909 and 1911, and then at
his speech on nationalism given at the Zionist Congress of 1921.

THE CULTURAL BACKGROUND
OF BUBER'S GERMANY

It is appropriate to begin with several introductory remarks
on Buber's place within Germany's cultural tradition before

the First World War. While Buber was born in Poland into a wealthy Jewish family, he went to Germany as a student, became familiar with German philosophy, entered deeply into German culture, and actively participated in the intellectual debates in the Germany of his time. His language, his poetic prose, was universally admired.

The scholars of Buber's work tell us that he was greatly influenced by two intellectual trends in turn-of-the-century Germany: the malaise of modernity shared by many German artists, writers, and intellectuals, and the so-called *Lebens-philosophie*, which emphasized the priority of life over form and structure. The sociological work that analysed the malaise of modernity was Ferdinand Toennies' famous book, *Gemein-schaft und Gesellschaft* (1887),[2] which contrasted the shared values and cultural rootedness characteristic of traditional communities (*Gemeinschaft*) with the abstract rationalism and isolating individualism characteristic of modern, industrial society (*Gesellschaft*). The loss of roots, Toennies showed, produced the decline of social solidarity and the waning of religious sentiment. His book was read by many as a lament over the modernization of German society taking place at that time, even if he himself did not see his own work in that way. He looked upon "community" and "society" as heuristic concepts that allowed social scientists to investigate the degree to which a concrete society reflected the rationality mediated by modern institutions and to what extent this society still preserved the communities and values proper to the earlier culture. Still, the book explained to many Germans and other Europeans why they felt so deeply alienated from the culture emerging from the three rationalizing trends operative in society, industrialization, commercialization, and bureaucratization. These Europeans lamented that the institutions in which they were forced to live did not correspond to their cultural and spiritual aspirations. Buber fully shared this malaise of modernity.

The idea, let me add, that modernity, by giving priority to technological or instrumental reason, transformed traditional society, relativized all values, fostered utilitarianism, and promoted the cult of the individual became an important theme in sociological literature. Max Weber's work on the cultural impact of modern bureaucracy concluded that the domination of instrumental reason would lead to the disenchantment of the world and the death of humanism.[3] George Lukacs introduced this critique of modernity into Marxist thought. Frankfurt School Critical Theory further developed the Weberian critique and argued that the contemporary form of Enlightenment, exclusive reliance on instrumental reason, was the great obstacle to human liberation as envisaged by the original Enlightenment. The Weberian critique has remained a major inspiration in critical sociology in all parts of the world.[4]

In the days of Martin Buber, one intellectual response to the culture of alienation was the *Lebensphilosophie*, a philosophical approach that recognized the creativity of human life and its capacity to transcend and reshape inherited forms or institutions. In Germany, the best-known among these philosophers was Wilhelm Dilthey, under whom Martin Buber had studied; in France it was Henri Bergson. Buber was also a personal friend of Georg Simmel, a German sociologist who agreed with the Weberian critique, yet resolutely refused to despair over the arrival of modernity. Simmel believed that the irrepressible spirit incarnate in human life had the capacity to overcome the older forms and structures that had become obstacles to human growth. Life was ever creative. Yet because life must ever reconcretize itself in forms and concepts, the dynamic process of deconstruction and reconstruction would never cease. History would remain a scene of conflict between the new and the old.

It is possible to situate existentialist philosophers in this intellectual context. While these thinkers were unhappy with the impersonal, objective, and alienating relationships produced by modern society – the "man" of Heidegger or the "I-it" of Buber – they also believed that personal choice, in fidelity to the human vocation, could lift people out of their societal framework and empower them to create a more authentic way of existence. Life freely affirmed leads to transcendence.

At the turn of the century Buber was profoundly alienated from modern society. He saw no value in bourgeois existence. He believed that not only in Germany but all over Europe thoughtful people were experiencing a profound malaise because the institutions in which they lived were at odds with the cultural values they had inherited and through which they defined their humanity. Buber here echoed the Weberian critique. He also held that Jews experienced this alienation more than other people. Why? Because Jews were deeply divided between the land, culture, and institutions in which they now lived and their own spiritual roots and social inheritance. Buber, as we shall see, never explained the malaise of Jewish existence in terms of the antisemitism to which Jews were exposed.

At this time of his life, Buber yearned for the personal liberation of Jews and other people through the experience of unity between their spiritual roots and their societal institutions. He came to believe that the personal power to transcend middle-class culture was offered and made available in God's revelation to the people of Israel. He tells us that when he first heard of the Zionist movement, founded a few years earlier, he greatly rejoiced. "The first impetus to my liberation came from Zionism, I can only intimate what it meant for me: the restoration of connection, the renewal taking root in the community."[5]

BEFORE WORLD WAR I: THREE SPEECHES ON JUDAISM

In three speeches on Judaism delivered in Prague between 1909 and 1911, Buber offered his first interpretation of Zionist nationalism.[6] He was invited to speak by a group of young Jews, artists and intellectuals, who were estranged from the religious and cultural traditions of their parents' or grandparents' generation. These young men had become secular. At the same time, they were ill at ease in the bourgeois society to which they now belonged, in part because they experienced discrimination and in part because they felt they were becoming individualists and utilitarians like the rest of the middle class. These young men were deeply moved by Martin Buber, and many became his friends and later his collaborators.

At the very outset of these speeches, Buber explains that the Jews are a nation and at the same time more than a nation, for they are defined by a unique relationship to the Eternal One. Yet it would be a mistake, he continues, to dwell on the spiritual dimension without appropriate attention to concrete Jewish history, the succession of generations, and the great events that had shaped their common destiny. Jewish identity is defined by the spirit and the flesh. The community of the dead, the living, and the as-yet unborn constitute the collectivity which grounds the Jewish self and defines its human vocation. "The past of his people is his personal memory, the future of his people is his personal task."[7]

Since Jewish existence has both a spiritual and a bodily dimension, Jews cannot escape their dividedness while living in countries founded by other nations. Jews can experience their liberation only in Zion; only there will they be able to experience the unity between spiritual roots and societal institutions. Buber argues against Jews who – like his friend, Georg Simmel – want to preserve the Jewish spirit while seeking assimilation to German society. In making his point, Buber uses a vocabulary that has become unacceptable today. Liberation can come about, he says, "only when the homeland where he grew up is also the homeland of his blood, when the language and the ways in which he grew up are at the same time the language and ways of his blood. ... This is not the situation of the Jews, especially of Western Jews ... The Jew is divided, his substance embodying his origin is banished into loneliness."[8]

The language of blood as the substance of Jewishness is disturbing. Buber writes,

Blood is a deep-rooted nurturing force within the individual, the deepest layers of our being are determined by blood, our innermost thinking and our will are coloured by it.[9]

Blood is the deepest, most potent stratum of our being ... [it] affects all we feel, do and think, ... implanted by the chain of fathers and mothers, by their nature and their fate, their deeds and their sufferings. It is time's great heritage that we bring with us into the world ... This chain goes back to the prophets ... The national prototype is the struggle of the prophets against the people's straying inclination ... In our longing for a pure and unified life we hear the sound of all that which once awaked the great Essene and the early Christian movement.[10]

What did blood mean for Buber? He had no sympathy for the racial theories of the nineteenth century which located the greatness or the negative potential of a people in the biological inheritance of its blood. Buber's biographer reports that at the Nuremberg trials, the Nazi philosopher Alfred Rosenberg and his defense lawyer appealed to Buber's use of the term blood to demonstrate that racial theories are not necessarily anti-semitic.[11] A reader familiar with Buber's work recognizes that what he meant by blood was the cultural continuity created by the chain of generations, perpetuating in words and gestures a way of being and the sense of sharing a common fate. Blood for the young Buber was the bodily aspect of the spiritual. He believed, as the above quotation suggests, that this bodily-spiritual continuity was present in Jesus of Nazareth and his religious movement, before the Christian Church interpreted him in a manner at odds with Jewish tradition.

The drama of Jews in Western society, according to Buber, is the deep schism between the world of impressions and the world of substance, between environment and blood, between the memory of a lifetime and the memory of millennia, between the objectives of society and the task of realizing their Jewish potential. Yet Buber does not ask Jews to reject the modern world. He recognizes that the Jews whom he is addressing have already assimilated its spirit; they have been partially shaped by it; in fact, they constitute a cultural mixture. Their task, he tells them, is to become the master, not the servant of this mixture – an echo of Simmel's *Lebensphilosophie*. Jews have to learn to say yes to themselves in the choice between environment and blood. For Buber this yes affirms at one and the same time the self and the entire people.

The unity between the Jew and his people moved Buber to use mystical language. "The Jew will feel that he is the people within himself. We suffer with the poor and oppressed. … Yet it is not together with them that I suffer; I am suffering their tribulation. My soul is not by the side of my people; my soul is my people."[12] This quotation reveals that Buber's nationalist passion is not simply a response to the malaise of modernity but also a compassionate reaction to the oppression and exclusion inflicted upon the Jews in Eastern and, to a lesser degree at that time, in Western Europe. We shall see in the next chapter that when Gandhi was challenged by his critics, he also justified his nationalism by invoking his solidarity with the poor and humiliated masses of India.

It is the lot of Jews, Buber continues, to have to affirm themselves as a people under most difficult circumstances: they have lost their land, their common language, and their national identity. Yet in their spiritual wrestling to be faithful to their substance, Jews resemble other nations, for they too must wrestle, even if under more fortunate circumstances, for fidelity to their deepest vocation. Buber here invokes the biblical myth of the fall, the conflict between good and evil, and the subjective division of the human heart. He proposes that in the Jewish people, because of their historical exclusion, this divided heart, this doubleness, entails contradictory impulses, the most exalted aspirations and the most debased: he mentions the love of truth versus crude mendacity and sacrificial love versus wilful egoism. We Jews, he states, must confront this doubleness, repent of it, try to overcome it, and in doing so become truly one, internally united. In this yearning for redemption, we Jews are the representatives of humankind. The Jewish vocation is to strive for unity, unity in the individual person, unity within the people, unity among the separated nations, unity between humans and their natural habitat, and unity between God and the world. Buber saw Jewish nationalism as serving the reconciliation of humanity.

Contemporary commentators have suggested that Buber's "romantic yearning for wholeness" was derived not so much from Judaism as from the German idealistic tradition going back to Jacob Böhme and earlier still to Nicholas of Cusa. Yet Buber himself was convinced that he was faithful to an authentically Jewish tradition, Prophetic Judaism. He explains that Prophetic Judaism is the religious tradition constituted during two periods in Hebrew history. The first period embraces the Exodus in which God rescued the Hebrews from external oppression and the Covenant in which God obliged them to internal justice; the second comprises the classical Hebrew prophets of the eighth and seventh century BCE, through whom God recalled Israel to social justice and care for the poor, clarified Israel's mission in the world, and promised the eventual reconciliation of the nations in peace and justice.

In his speeches at Prague, Buber announces that the moment of Jewish renewal has come: the rebirth of Prophetic

Judaism. With the foundation of the Zionist movement "something sudden and immense" is occurring in the Jewish community. The divine summons to unity, he tells his audience, is beginning to express itself in a renewed existence of the Jewish people, not just a rejuvenation or revival, but a genuine and total renewal.

Speaking from his commitment to Prophetic Judaism, Buber offers a severe criticism of Judaism's existing religious traditions, Orthodoxy and Reform. His radicalism must have offended many practising Jews at the time. Orthodox Judaism, Buber believes, is caught in the past, restricted to ritual observance, confined to repetition, and thus opposed to a new and bold response to God's call in the present. In his eyes Reform Judaism does not fare any better. The keen desire to conform to bourgeois culture makes Reformed Jews rationalize their beliefs and reduce to a minimum the traditional ritual. What they offer, Buber says, is "negation and nothing but negation."[13] Buber believes that for all Jews, be they Orthodox or Reformed, the hour, the historical moment, has come calling for their conversion to a new self-perception, a new rootedness in the prophetic tradition, a new affirmation of their peoplehood, and a new turn to the living God.

Buber was critical of the leaders of the Zionist movement. He disagreed with Theodor Herzl, the founder of the movement, who understood Zionism in political terms and appealed to kings and princes to secure a homeland for the Jews in Palestine. Herzl did not see Zionism as a call to spiritual conversion, nor did he announce the return of the Jews to the Promised Land as the beginning of a religious and cultural renaissance. Buber had more sympathy for Ahad Haam, a Zionist leader from Eastern Europe, who envisaged the creation of an original Jewish culture in Palestine based on biblical tradition and freed from bourgeois principles. Haam strongly believed in the cultural resourcefulness of the

Jews: once settled in their own land, they would be able to set up their own social institutions and enter upon a Jewish renaissance. What greatly disturbed Buber was that Haam was not a believer: he interpreted the biblical story of Israel's past and its promised destiny in cultural, not religious terms. Haam rejected Israel's choseness. By contrast, Buber was deeply convinced that without reliance on the Eternal One, Jews could not succeed in constituting themselves as an internally reconciled people serving the cause of justice. Buber held that no people, no human community, could successfully realize a social project defined by love, justice, and peace without a trusting reliance on God: "Redemption does not come from humans."[14]

According to Buber's prophetic interpretation, Judaism is more than a religion and more than a nation; it is the spiritual ground of a constant striving for overcoming divisions and achieving ever more perfect realizations of human unity. Judaism is neither an ethical nor a religious realm, but the unity between the two. Nor are the national and the social concerns separate principles. "Nationalism as an isolated view of life and socialism as isolated view of life are equally alien to Judaism."[15] In Zionism, the national principle is the substance and the social principle the task. The destiny of Zion is not to be a purely political reality, not another one of the innumerable states devoid of spiritual substance, where spirit and people are separated, both languishing, the one as a form of intellectualism removed from life and the other as the masses remote from ideas. Zion must not become a community where possessing replaces being, where mutual exploitation replaces cooperation, and where people refuse to annihilate one another only because they fear and need each other. This yearning for redemption exists in all peoples, but thanks to God's gift of Scripture this longing exists in the Jewish people with special intensity.

In the three speeches Buber reveals himself as a radical. He calls for a total turning. Jews are confronted by an either/or: either they choose to renew their faith or Judaism will disappear. Buber has been compared to Søren Kierkegaard who in the mid-nineteenth century accused Christianity of having lost its rootedness in the Gospel and demanded an existentialist conversion of individuals to an inward faith. Buber's call for an existentialist conversion is addressed to an entire people. It has been argued that his radical formulation of Prophetic Judaism reflected, in part at least, the *Lebensphilosophie* mentioned above, attributing spirit-filled life with the power to transcend static forms and break forth into newness. Hans Kohn, one of the young men whom Buber met in Prague and who joined him in the cause of Zionism, would later write: "Our Zionism was not a reaction to persecution, but under the influence of the German thought of the period, a search for roots ... a turning inward towards the supposed centre of our true self, which dated back, so we believed, over 2000 years to biblical times."[16]

What is surprising in Buber's three speeches on Judaism is his support for back-to-roots nationalism without denouncing the chauvinist nationalist movements of his day, some of which were agents of xenophobia and antisemitism. He expressed his sympathy for Charles Péguy who summoned France to a renewed national self-understanding, but did not mention the anti-democratic, Catholic nationalism massively supported in France at the same time.[17] Buber focused on the spiritual dimension of nationalism. Despite his talk about blood, he did not think of Zionism simply as the self-affirmation of an ethnic community: for him Zionism involved a spiritual conversion, a turning away from bourgeois society and a turning to Prophetic Judaism. Since Buber accepted the Weberian critique of modernity, he believed that Zionism was a witness offered to other nations, calling them to recover their own spiritual roots. Zionism was a service to humanity. It was only after World War I that Buber explored the negative potential of nationalism.

It is worth adding at this point that Jewish nationalism was accepted only by a small minority of Jews at the beginning of the twentieth century. Most Orthodox Jews looked upon the Jewish people primarily as a religious community. The Jews in Eastern Europe understood themselves as constituting a Yiddish-speaking people: they even enjoyed a certain cultural nationalism promoting their institutions, literature, and music, intent on preserving their collective identity. Reformed Jews in Western Europe tended to favour cultural assimilation: their Jewish identity lay in their biblically based, prophetic mission to give witness to God or simply to truth and justice in the countries to which they belonged. For some this meant commitment to liberal ideals, for others to socialist goals. Assimilated Jews tended to react with silence or even hostility to the Zionist claim. Well-known authors, Stephan Zweig, Alfred Döblin, and Lion Feuchtwanger among them, totally repudiated the idea that Jews were a people in a political sense. Some of them regarded Zionism as racist. In the twenties, Feuchtwanger called it "*ein jüdische Art von Hitlerei*," a Jewish form of Hitlerism.[18] It was only after World War II and the Holocaust that the great majority of Jews became supporters of Zionism and, after 1948, the State of Israel.

AFTER WORLD WAR I:
THE SPEECH AT THE ZIONIST CONGRESS

In his speech to the 12th Zionist Congress of 1921, meeting in Karlsbad, Martin Buber spoke about nationalism in a new tone. His commentators have explained this change in terms of Buber's philosophical evolution from his early existentialism to the more mature relational, interdependent understanding of the human being. Moving away from the idea that people constitute their being through personal conversion, Buber began to recognize that people come to be through their interaction with the community into which they are born and in which they live. Our consciousness, our language, our feelings, our entire personal being is generated by our participation in a family, a community, and a nation. In this social process personal responsibility remains intact, for we are free to respond to these relations in accordance with our own choice. Yet what we can never change is that we have been shaped by the interaction with this family, this community, and this nation. We are inserted into humanity not as individuals, but as members of a nation. Nationalism has here an anthropological foundation.

That humans are constituted by participation in their social matrix is an idea widely held among sociologists. It is the central insight of Émile Durkheim's important scientific achievement.[19] Not only are we made by the society into which we are born, but even our self-understanding is mediated by the symbols of this society. Later sociologists preferred the term "socialization": humans enter upon their humanity through integration into a social matrix. For Durkheim this social determination did not obliterate human freedom. On the contrary, modern society, he argued, creates people as citizens and as such summons them to assume personal responsibility.

Buber's defense of nationalism after World War I is based on what I shall call the Durkheimian argument. We shall meet both the Weberian critique and the Durkheimian argument in the other authors to be studied in this book, and we shall have occasion to ask ourselves whether these two principles are complementary or in contradiction with one another.

The other change in Buber's treatment of nationalism is his decision to face nationalism's negative potential. He is greatly disturbed by the arrogant and aggressive nationalism that, he thinks, has emerged during and after the Great War, and he is also worried about the orientation taken by the Zionist movement in the same period. Buber honours the Arab community in Palestine and respects their struggle to protect their national identity. After incidents of Arab violence against Jewish settlers, Buber fears that the outrage over this is pushing Zionism toward an arrogant and aggressive nationalism. His speech on nationalism given at the Zionist Congress in 1921, which was not well received,[20] clarified his understanding of Zionism and warned that the movement, begun in a prophetic spirit, might end as a self-regarding, exclusivist nationalism undermining the substance of Judaism.

Buber begins his speech with the remark that "a degenerate kind of nationalism has of late begun to spread in Judaism."[21] Still, he continues to defend ethical nationalism as the source of cultural renewal. Reflecting on the origin of modern nationalism – something he did not do in the three speeches – he recalls the political struggle of nations against their subjugation within the feudal-aristocratic order, the struggle of which the French Revolution became the powerful symbol. These nations, Buber continues, became keenly aware of what they were lacking, such as territorial unity, internal reconciliation, and economic independence. To overcome these lacks, nationalist movements created the modern, bourgeois state with its centralized, mechanistic, and bureaucratic institutions. The all-powerful and self-serving state, Buber argues, is one cause of the ambivalence of nationalist movements.

A second cause of this ambivalence lies in the psychological insecurity of the European populations. Buber holds that the break-up of Christian Europe at the Reformation and the shattering of the age-old feudal civilization by bourgeois revolutions left the people of Europe without any solid cultural and symbolic ground on which to stand. The cultural sweep of science and technology, which leaves unanswered fundamental human questions, only intensifies people's insecurities. In this situation, many people find in the nationalist movements an answer to their search for meaning. Buber argues that seeking in the finite order of history answers belonging to the realm of transcendence tempts these people to make the nation the highest good and the ultimate norm.

The modern nation-state ruling over a people willing to entrust it with their souls created totally new conditions for the exercise of power. "In the individual, the original feeling of allegiance to a people, alive in the depth of his soul long before the modern national awareness, changed from a creative power to a challenging will-to-power of the individual as a member of a community. The group-egoism of the individual emerged in its modern form."[22] Personal selflessness can go hand in hand with collective self-centredness. While Buber recognizes political power as a good and necessary public faculty, namely the capacity of a government to act and realize the rich potential of the nation, he distinguishes political power from will-to-power, that is the voracious desire to seize and establish power so as to become more powerful than others. Insisting on one's own rights, one violates the rights of others. Buber laments what he calls power hysteria. He proposes that in any political movement the line of demarcation between genuine and false nationalism cannot be defined once and for all, but demands ongoing critical reflection. Modern nationalism, he insists, is in constant danger of slipping into a power hysteria that would abolish collective responsibility because it draws a clear line of demarcation between what is legitimate and what is not.

In the same speech Buber offered clear definitions of what he means by people, nation, and nationalism. A people, he now corrects himself, is not necessarily defined by common ethnic origin. A people is not always a fusion of kindred stems; sometimes it is a fusion of unrelated stems. What defines a people is a common fate. Certain historical events are capable of uniting groups of people in a new community fused into a whole by a dramatic fate experienced in common. This newly moulded collectivity now redefines kinship among its members and creates its own original cultural development. To ensure its continuity in time such a people tend to oppose marriage to outsiders. Yet what is more important for the unity and creativity of the people and their historical continuity is the commemoration of the fateful founding events in stories and public festivals. The celebration of these memories also allows the integration of new members, derived from other strains, who are willing to accept the common story, share the common fate, and learn the people's language and way of life. Yet for the great majority, membership is by birth. Buber calls a people a "natural" community, to distinguish it from the "symbolic" community of the church. The Jewish people are a "natural" community. A people survives biologically, but – Buber now insists – cannot be fitted into a biological category.

What is a nation? Buber argues that a people becomes a nation when it becomes aware of being different from other peoples, begins to act on the basis of this awareness, and gradually sees itself as responsible for its future. A people becomes a nation when it acquires a historical consciousness. An evolution of this kind takes place when a people is challenged by internal conflicts and transformations or by external events like land conquests, invasions, or massive immigration.

What is nationalism? Here Buber returns to his above-mentioned interpretation. Nationalism is the reaction of a nation to a lack, an insufficiency, or a wound from which it suffers. It is a movement in national life that wrestles against a social illness. This illness may be caused by external forces that limit political or economic autonomy, or by internal forces such as rootlessness and social amnesia and assimilation to a purely utilitarian culture. Nationalism is first of all a spiritual movement – on this point, we note, Buber has not changed his mind. A nationalist movement, he argues, has two possible historical outcomes: either it overcomes these insufficiencies, heals these wounds, and then gradually fades away, or it turns into a permanent principle, exceeds its original purpose, and displaces the spontaneous life of the nation. In the first case, nationalism applies the unwritten "*droit des nations*" to a particular people and in doing so serves the pacification of humankind, while in the second case, nationalism transgresses its legitimate object, produces arrogance and aggressivity, and becomes a harmful cultural and political force in the world. Destined to heal an illness, nationalism can become itself a grave and complicated illness. It is quite possible that a people would gain the right for which they strove and yet fail to regain their health. Why? Because their nationalism has become prideful and arbitrary, distorting their spiritual and cultural tradition. Buber calls this a false nationalism.

The leaders of a nationalist movement, even more than their followers, are obliged to engage in continual critical reflection in order to define a clear line between genuine and arbitrary nationalism. The distinction involves a choice between life and death, for it is possible that a people's cultural spontaneity, nourished by the primordial forces of its historical existence, may be strangled by an administrative apparatus bent on gaining arbitrary power. Nationalism becomes self-destructive and destructive of others when it refuses to acknowledge its supranational purpose of serving the reconciliation of humanity. Buber reiterates the viewpoint expressed in his three speeches before the war that the nation is never the highest good, that it is not an end in itself, that it has no right to think of itself as superior to others, that it is meant to recognize the dignity of other nations, cooperate with them, and together with them work for justice and peace in the world. Nationalism loses its spiritual grounding if it prompts people to group-egoism and collective self-elevation. There exists no hierarchical ordering among the nations because God has created them as equals marvellously different from one another, yet destined to join in the building of a peaceful world. "The moment a national ideology makes the nation an end in itself, it annuls its own right to live, it grows sterile."[23]

In the last part of the speech before the Zionist Congress, Buber applies his ethical theory of nationalism to the Jewish people. The Jews, he insists, are not simply a nation, they are at the same time a community of faith. Jewry has an altogether particular character: it claims the rights and privileges due to any people, and at the same time it sees itself as a chosen people, a people elected by God, not to enjoy a superior status from which to look down upon others, but to give witness to the Creator and the Creator's purpose for humanity and the cosmos. Buber reminds his audience of the harsh teaching uttered by the biblical prophets that we, the chosen people, shall forfeit our destiny if we boast of our election instead of living up to it, and turn it into a privilege instead of obeying it as a command.

Still, the nationalism of the Jewish people is fully legitimate. It is a nation with a land of its own that has lost its country, and a nation with a spiritual tradition in danger of losing it under the impact of foreign cultures and modern Western rationalism. Judaism can fulfil its task in the world only if it becomes grounded again in the land of its origin and embodied in institutions appropriate to its own genius. Buber, speaking in 1921, sees the beginning of a Jewish renaissance in the Jewish settler communities in Palestine. He does not mention a Jewish state. What threatens this genuine Jewish nationalism, he continues, is the waning of faith in God and the desire for assimilation, in order to make the Jewish people one of the nations of the world. Why is this dangerous? Because when the sense of God's presence is lost, Jewish nationalism exposes itself to the temptation of all nationalist movements, namely to make the nation the highest good, and in the name of that good, to become arrogant and aggressive in regard to other nations. Thinking of the strained relations of the Jewish settlers with the Palestinian population, Buber pleads with the Zionist Congress "to save Jewish nationalism from the error of making an idol of the nation." "The nationalistic crisis in Judaism," he continues, "is in sharp relief in the pattern of the nationalistic crisis of current world history."[24]

In his speech of 1921 to the Zionist Congress Buber developed a dialectical understanding of nationalism, in which the ideas of his earlier three speeches have their place. He saw nationalism as a spiritual movement summoning a people to cultural or, if need be, political and economic self-determination; at the same time he recognized that nationalism is always tempted to abandon its spiritual grounding, make the nation an end in itself, and become an agent of cultural and political domination. Which of these two aspects deserves the greater emphasis depends on the historical situation. Speaking in Prague to discouraged and alienated Jews before World War I Buber offered spiritual conversion and Zionist passion as the answer to their malaise, while speaking in Karlsbad to the Zionist Congress after the war he analysed the dangers threatening Jewish nationalism.

IN SUBSEQUENT YEARS

Buber remained faithful to this dialectical approach. In a public letter to Gandhi written in 1939, when Buber had moved to Palestine, he offered a passionate defense of Jewish nationalism.[25] Gandhi, having been asked to make a public statement on the Jewish-Palestinian conflict, expressed his admiration for Jewish religion and Jewish tradition, but concluded that the Jews were immigrants in Palestine – like the

Indians living in South Africa – and must, as immigrants, create their community and seek social justice in the country that belongs to the resident population. Buber replied with an ardent defense of the Jewish claim to the Promised Land, even as he acknowledged that the Arab population had an equally strong claim to the same territory. He was confident that through dialogue, cooperation, and friendship a compromise of mutual recognition could be achieved.

Writing in those days, Buber also offered his reflections on the fascist nationalism raging in Europe.

Something without precedent is taking place in this era: some of the nationalist egoisms which have been held in check by Christianity as by a common and supreme truth have freed themselves not only from Christianity, but from all inhibitions whatever. In their eyes, truth is nothing more than the function of the nation and the "prince" proclaims himself as God.[26]

In subsequent years Buber continued to criticize the leadership of the Zionist movement and, after 1948, the government of the State of Israel, whenever they violated what he regarded as the norm of Prophetic Judaism and endangered the substance of Israel's spiritual tradition. Engagement in a nationalist movement is always a risk. Buber believed that Zionism is worth this risk because it is the spiritual and bodily realization of Israel's divine vocation.

It is worth mentioning that Buber was greatly troubled by the ambiguity of the modern state. In the early days of Zionism he had hoped that the Jewish community in Palestine would be able to transcend the institutions of bourgeois society, including the state and the capitalist system. For Buber primacy was to be given to the social. People living and working together, engaging in conversation, becoming friends, discovering the values they share and defining their common interests – society was to be built from the bottom up. Buber applied this approach to the national economy and developed his concept of cooperative socialism;[27] and he applied the same principle to the formation of the state.

Buber opposed the creation of the Jewish state by the United Nations. In 1947 he lamented "the current exaggeration of politics."[28] The Jewish community in Palestine did not need, he suggested, a state in which to be sovereign. What he wanted was cooperation within a joint bi-national socio-political entity, in which each side was responsible for the particular matters pertaining to it, and both together participated in ordering their common concern. Only mutual respect and active cooperation between Jews and Arabs could resolve the Palestinian conflict. A state, even a federal state, was acceptable only if it were a political institution that perfected and stabilized existing forms of social interaction. A state imposed by political power from above would distort the social initiatives and cultural talents of any nation, including the Jewish nation. Buber believed it was "a fundamental error"[29] to partition Palestine and seek a political solution for a problem that was at bottom social and cultural.

Once the Jewish state was created Buber remained in critical solidarity with it. Until his death he remained an eloquent spokesman for Prophetic Judaism in the State of Israel.

3
Mahatma Gandhi's Ethic
of Nationalism

Prior to the arrival of the British, the peoples of the Indian sub-continent were ruled by regional dynasties. As in European feudalism, political power was in the hands of the princes, and people defined their collective identity through loyalty to their prince. The Indian lands were inhabited by many national or ethnic communities, heirs of different cultures and different languages. As a British colony, the peoples of India were for the first time placed under a single sovereign administrative power. They were subject to the same legal system and pacified by the same military strategy. Railroads, postal services, newspapers, industrial development, and other innovations brought by the British produced among the Indian elites a new sense of an all-Indian identity. Since they now spoke English, many of them having been educated in Britain, they were able to communicate among one another in the same language. Common interests and increased communication gave India a sense of nationhood. From their Western education the educated groups took the ideas of freedom, justice, and self-determination. Yet they also made the painful discovery that the same West inflicted upon them the heavy burden of racial discrimination. These men belonging to the elite began to see India as a nation in the modern sense, in other words as a sovereign people with the right to overthrow its domination by a foreign empire and establish its own independent state. The creation of the Indian National Congress in 1885 can be taken as the beginning of a Western-style nationalist movement in India.

It has often been argued that Britain's colonization of India created the social forces that eventually brought forth the Indian nation. One historian writes, "Before the British conquest, the concept of membership in a permanent political order embracing and involving all seems to have been unknown to the inhabitants of India."[1] Other historians emphasize the cultural unity of ancient origin inherited by the peoples of India.

Indian nationalists have been divided into Moderates and Extremists.[2] The Moderates regarded English rule as providential, having brought to India modern ideas, such as self-government, equal justice for all, an efficient economy, and the separation of government from religion. These men were modernizers, even if they were in disagreement about the role of industrialization in India. They hoped that their political struggle at home, supported by progressive voices among Liberals and Labourites in Britain, would eventually persuade the British parliament to recognize Indian self-rule. While they respected the British legal system, they objected to the laws that humiliated Indians and willingly went to prison for disobeying them. Yet they disapproved of all forms of violence and hence opposed the Extremists.

The Extremists were hostile to the British. They supported the spiritual revival of Hinduism among the people as a source of resistance to foreign rule. While they agreed with the Moderates that English should become India's common language, they put great emphasis on the vernacular tongues. They advocated greater unity between the educated and the peasants in the regions of India, based on the renewal of Hindu religion and the cultivation of the regional language. Whereas the Moderates fostered Hindu-Muslim cooperation, the Extremists put an almost exclusive emphasis on Hindu solidarity. They tried to reduce India's dependency on Britain by boycotting foreign articles, advocating the use of Indian-made goods, fostering indigenous education, and creating alternative administrative structures. These men were often exiled or jailed. Many of them believed that violence in some form was necessary to chase the British out of India.

Steering between these two political trends, Mahatma Gandhi worked out his own ethico-religious nationalism. He shared with the Moderates the horror of violence and the desire for Hindu-Muslim solidarity; and he had a certain affinity for the policies of the Extremists, especially the call for religious renewal uniting the educated with the people and the search for strategies that would make Indians more independent of the empire.

The spiritual journey of Mahatma Gandhi (1869–1948) is well known. He was born in the region of Gujarat and brought up by his mother in the gentle, ascetical, non-violent "*ahimsa*" tradition of Hinduism. When he went to England at the age of eighteen to study law, he was impressed by several Western spiritual ideas, such as the teachings of Jesus and the pacifist anarchism of Kropotkin and Tolstoy. When he returned to India three years later he had great sympathy for the Britain he had encountered. The great shock of his life was his experience of violent racism in South Africa. He had been invited to that country by a Muslim Indian who wanted the support of a lawyer, and when Gandhi saw that the South African Indian community needed leadership in its struggle for justice, he decided to stay. He remained in South Africa for twenty years. It was there that he discovered an all-Indian solidarity, embracing both Hindus and Muslims and reaching beyond the divisions of language, culture, and caste that played such an important role in India. The experience of racial oppression turned Gandhi into a political radical. When he returned to India in 1914, dressed as a peasant, it did not take him long to become the leading spokesman of the Indian National Congress.

To understand Gandhi's nationalism we shall examine the pamphlet entitled *Hind Swaraj* (Indian home rule or self-government), which he wrote in 1909 and which, in spite of its vehement polemics, he continued to regard as a true expression of his nationalism.[3] In 1921, when Gandhi organized a nation-wide campaign of non-cooperation with the British, he was challenged by Rabindranath Tagore, the great Indian poet, who in the name of international solidarity objected to Gandhi's nationalism. We shall examine the famous debate between these two great Indian personalities.

HIND SWARAJ

This radical pamphlet, written in English, records the conversation of the author with a sceptical friend who raises difficulties and demands clarifications. In this conversation Gandhi explains his unqualified rejection of the modern civilization created by the British and the European nations. He radicalizes the Weberian critique of modernity that had influenced Martin Buber.[4] Gandhi draws upon British critics of modern civilization, especially radical Tories, who judged contemporary society in the light of an idealized image of the past. He mentions in particular Edward Carpenter's *Civilization: Its Cause and Cure*, published in 1884 and then many times reprinted, which had encouraged him to look upon civilization as a disease.

What then is civilization? Civilization, in Gandhi's definition, makes people look upon bodily welfare as the object of their lives. The society created by capitalism, democracy, science, and technology is oriented toward the promotion of material progress, and is inevitably accompanied by selfishness, greed, and the love of pleasure. In such a society people cannot achieve their spiritual destiny. Still, Gandhi continues, contemporary philosophers and politicians offer ethical arguments in favour of modern civilization: they tell us that wealth, comfort, and pleasure are worthy human goals, to which eventually all members of society ought to have access. Gandhi comments, "After twenty years' experience, I have come to the conclusion that immorality is often taught in the name of morality."[5] Civilization, he thinks, is an unmitigated evil because it undermines the human vocation to lead a spiritual life. In other texts he goes so far as calling modern civilization satanic.[6]

Civilization, it should be noted, is not due to a peculiar fault of the English. Gandhi insists on this. Civilization is presently degrading and ruining all the nations of Europe. The desire for material progress and the vices associated with the effort to achieve it are presently undermining the ethical traditions the nations have inherited. If I understand him correctly, Gandhi designates as civilization the process which sociologists refer to as "modernization." Gandhi asks his Indian readers not to blame the English for their effort to modernize Indian society, but rather to feel sorry for them.[7] The English, heirs of an ancient ethical culture, must be pitied for the disease that has taken hold of them. Their present civilization is self-destructive: it extinguishes virtue and thus prepares the collapse of society.

Gandhi tells us that in his own language, Gujarati, the word for civilization means "good conduct." True civilization is the mode of conduct that sends people on the path of duty. "Doing one's duty is the same as observing morality, and observing morality means to attain mastery over one's mind and one's passions."[8] True civilization leads people to a life of discipline, wisdom, and compassion.

India is superior to the Western nations, Gandhi argues, because it is unshakeably rooted in its spiritual tradition. India has nothing to learn from the West. Our Indian ancestors, he continues, recognized that humans are by nature restless birds. Since their desires and cravings are endless, humans who follow their passions are never satisfied and hence are forever disappointed and frustrated. Thus our ancestors set a limit to our indulgences. They saw that happiness was largely a mental condition. A man is not necessarily happy because he is rich, or unhappy because he is poor. Millions of people will always live in poverty. Observing all this, Gandhi continues, our ancestors dissuaded us from luxury and pleasures.

We have managed with the same kind of plough as existed thousands of years ago. We have retained the same kind of cottages that we had in former times and our indigenous education remains the same as before. We had no system of life-corroding competition. ... It was not that we did not know how to invent machinery, but our forefathers knew that, if we set our hearts after such things, we would become slaves and lose our moral fibre. They, therefore, after due deliberation decided that we should only do what we could with our hands and feet. They saw that our real happiness and health consisted in the proper use of our hands and feet.[9]

People then lived in villages, they had little to do with the princes and their courts; they sometimes suffered under burdens imposed on them by their rulers, but they were not dominated by them. They possessed *swaraj*: they enjoyed home rule because they were self-disciplined, modest, and happy. In the major parts of India that have not been touched by the modernization brought by the English and foolishly welcomed by Indian elites, the people in the villages still have *swaraj*, they are not dominated, they enjoy self-rule. *Swaraj* is primarily an ethical achievement. It is *swaraj* when we learn to rule ourselves. It is, therefore, in our hand.[10]

Gandhi does not deny that Indian cultural tradition included many forms of injustice, harmful especially to women and the lower castes. Yet he hoped that "the new spirit"[11] created by the joint struggle against the present evil of forced modernization would enable the people to reform their tradition in accordance with what was best and highest in it. Part of this reform was Gandhi's effort to obtain the religious, cultural, and legal assimilation of the lowest caste, the untouchables. All Indians are destined to enjoy *swaraj*.

The English occupation and its modernizing impact constitute the enemy against which the Indian people must be mobilized. Of course, if the English living in India are willing to become Indianized, that is if they want to join India's great spiritual tradition, they are most welcome. For Gandhi there is nothing racial or ethnic in Indian nationalism. He realized that India is made up of different peoples and different ethnic, religious, linguistic, and cultural communities. What unites all Indians, according to Gandhi, is the ancient tradition of Hinduism, the powerful ethico-religious culture that has influenced all Indian religious and cultural traditions, including Islam. Yet what Gandhi does not seem to recognize – we shall discuss this further on – is that conceiving India as a nation and mobilizing Indian nationalism are also, in part at least, products of modernizing ideas and institutions brought by Western civilization.

Gandhi is repelled by the idea, proposed by some Extremists, that British rule in India should be overcome by the force of arms. He rejects this for two reasons. First, if military power overthrew British rule and replaced it by the rule of the princes, the people of India would continue to suffer injustice. There are, Gandhi continues, Indian princes whose tyranny is greater than that of the British. *Swaraj* means that these princes must be resisted. True patriotism aims at the welfare of the whole people. If the English helped us, Gandhi adds, to become a more just society, we should welcome them. "If any Englishman dedicated his life to securing the freedom of India, resisting tyranny and serving the land, I should welcome that Englishman as an Indian."[12] Military power can never achieve *swaraj*. Second, if India were to arm itself against a major military power such as Britain, India would become Europeanized. India would have to accumulate capital, advance industrialization, and become a technological society, and in doing so end up in the pitiable situation in which Europe finds itself.

The struggle for the independence of India must be based on the self-rule of each citizen. Here Gandhi introduces the strategy of *satya/graha*, usually translated as truth-force or soul-force or passive resistance. "Passive resistance is a method of securing rights by personal suffering; it is the reverse of resistance by arms. When I refuse to do a thing that is repugnant to my conscience, I use soul-force."[13] Individuals who refuse to obey an unjust law and accept the penalty for this offer themselves as a sacrifice. When such passive resistance is practiced by a large group or even the masses, it paralyses the ruling power and becomes politically effective.

Passive resistance is an all-sided sword. It blesses him who uses it and him against whom it is used. Without drawing a drop of blood it produces far-reaching results. It never rusts and cannot be stolen. Competition between passive resisters does not exhaust ... It is strange that (there are some people who) consider this weapon to be a weapon merely of the weak.[14]

Another form of passive resistance is *swadeshi*, or non-cooperation with the ruling power. To oppose the imposition of unjust measures and affirm their right to self-determination, people may choose not to cooperate with British colonial power, for instance by refusing to be educated in English or to buy goods produced in England. *Swadeshi* calls for personal sacrifice since, by refusing to cooperate with the rulers who have access to rich resources, one takes on the burden of providing for oneself.

To be able to engage in passive resistance in any of its forms, Gandhi insists, people are in need of virtue. They must observe perfect chastity, adopt poverty, follow truth, and cultivate fearlessness.[15] Gandhi offers long explanations of what these virtues mean. Chastity assures self-discipline and mastery over desire; poverty cultivates detachment from things that are not necessities; love of truth gives people the soul-force to oppose their rulers, and fearlessness supports them in their non-violent resistance.

At the end of the pamphlet Gandhi summarizes the points he has made.

1. Real home-rule is self-rule or self-control. 2. The way to it is passive resistance: that is soul-force or love-force. 3. In order to exert this force *swadeshi* in every sense is necessary. 4. What we want to do should be done, not because we object to the English or we want to retaliate, but because it is our duty to do so. Thus supposing that the English remove the salt-tax, restore our money, give the highest post to Indians, withdraw the English troops, we shall certainly not use their machine-made goods, nor use the English language, nor many of their industries. It is worth noting that these things are, in their nature, harmful; hence we do not want them. I bear no enmity toward the English but I do toward their civilization.[16]

GANDHI'S ETHICAL NATIONALISM

In *Hind Swaraj*, Gandhi offers an original version of Indian nationalism that is distinct from the nationalism of the

Moderates and the Extremists. For him nationalism contains a double imperative: it aims at personal, religious transformation and at the creation of the political state. In this it resembles Martin Buber's Zionist nationalism. Like Buber's Zionism, Gandhi's nationalism is a cultural and political movement ruled by a strict religious ethic that seeks to protect the movement from opportunism, injustice, and violence, and to foster within it a sense of universal solidarity.

Yet Gandhi's rejection of modernization is more radical than Buber's critique of modern, individualistic, and utilitarian society, which the Jewish philosopher shared with many social thinkers of his day; in the previous chapter, we recalled the work of Ferdinand Toennies and Max Weber which spread this critique in German-speaking lands. Gandhi was also more radical than the earlier critics, the European Romantics, who lamented the arrival of industrialization and the creation of the modern state, and advocated the return to the communal and ethical social order inherited from European feudalism. Gandhi, we noted above, did not want a return to Indian feudalism. At the same time, Gandhi's rejection of modernity was so radical – he objected even to railways connecting the regions of India – that it is hard to believe that he was quite serious. A pamphlet, even when written for a just cause, is propaganda. It overdraws. Intending to persuade and mobilize vast numbers of people, its literary form includes exaggeration. In subsequent years, we are told, Gandhi corrected some of these exaggerations, while reaffirming the substance of his *Hind Swaraj*.

Let me add that the Gandhian imperative to reject Western-style technological development has been taken up at the present time by several scientists and activists in India and other southern countries that are wrestling with the massive problem of hunger and destitution.[17] These critics offer empirical evidence that borrowing the ideal of material progress and importing science and technology have not improved the lot of the majority of the population. On the contrary, development has undermined their culture and social cohesion, made them dependent on foreign imports, such as fertilizer and machinery, driven them into debt and ruin, and caused unexpected and unintended ecological damage. The Gandhian imperative to promote a subsistence economy located in village communities has retained its relevance.

Gandhi's strict ascetical and ethical demands sound shocking to Western ears. For the Mahatma virtue is primarily self-discipline and self-denial. The pamphlet does not make clear whether he proposes an ethic of duty, calling people to do the right thing as defined by their religious tradition, whatever the consequences, or an ethic of self-realization, calling people to find their true happiness beyond the allurements of power, wealth, and pleasure. Gandhi moves repeatedly from one to the other. He probably thought that a religious ethic has two inseparable dimensions, the divine summons demanding obedience and the divine presence promising blessedness.

The Western reader is disturbed by Gandhi's ethic of self-restraint since contemporary culture is oriented toward personal growth and material progress and is almost devoid of spiritual resources for self-limitation. We want a society that grants us the freedom to promote ourselves and live up to our own vision of self-development. The market, which has become the dominant institution, is a process of exchange where everyone tries to get the best deal. Even Judaism and Christianity, the religions of the West, have relaxed their disciplinary and ascetical demands and foster personal self-realization and principled participation in modern society. For most of us brought up in Western culture, Gandhi's ethic of self-sacrifice and self-limitation seems outrageous.

Still, even the Western Enlightenment tradition is not totally devoid of spiritual resources for personal self-restraint and universal solidarity. Immanuel Kant's formal ethics of obligation has a certain affinity with Gandhi's interpretation of Hindu morality. Kant argues that ethics are autonomous, rational, and self-imposed. How do I decide whether my actions are ethical? They are ethical if the principle guiding them can be universalized, in other words be applied as a behavioural guide by people anywhere in the world. Kant's rational norm can be regarded as a philosophical formulation of the traditional dictum "Do unto others what you want them to do unto you." According to Kantian ethics, the principle that guides consumption – personal consumption of foods and other goods and society's consumption of energy and natural resources – is ethical only if it can be applied to people and their societies in all parts of the world. Since Western consumption patterns cannot be universalized – universal application overreaches the globe's natural resources – and hence can only be sustained for a privileged minority, these patterns are unethical. Kant would agree with Gandhi that the ethical life in today's world demands self-restraint and the ability to be happy in limited material circumstances.

In his book *The Mahatma and Mother India*, Peter Brock mentions several aspects of Gandhi's nationalism that deserve critical attention. First, Gandhi attached great importance to a national interpretation of Indian history. Even though India was pluralistic, made up of peoples with different languages and cultures, Gandhi insisted that Indians were of the same "race," as it was called then,[18] or have the same "roots," as we would say today, grounded in the ancient Hindu culture that had influenced all of India's religions. The Indians thus constituted a nation or a people with the ethical right to self-rule or self-determination. Gandhi opposed the idea that the British presence in India and the resistance against it were the important events that had created the Indian nation. "I hold (this theory) to be a mistake. The English have taught us that we were not one nation before and that it will require centuries before we become one nation. This is without foundation. We were one nation before they came to India."[19] It was important for Gandhi that the study of Indian history reveal the cultural cohesion enjoyed by the Indians from time immemorial.[20] Some historians have suggested that in antiquity a certain political cohesion did exist among the peoples of India.

Many Englishmen, following the ideas of Lord Macauley, believed that the Indians were incapable of governing themselves and that, therefore, British rule in India rendered an important service to the indigenous population. This claim justifying British imperialism was refuted by several historians – in particular Max Müller and Henry Sumner Maine[21] – who uncovered the structure of the ancient Indian civilization with its self-governing villages. Gandhi relied on their research in his praise of Indian greatness. In *Hind Swaraj*, he listed the past achievements of Indians and created his own version of Indian history. Sometimes he even argued that Indian civilization was richer and more spiritual than any other in the world. He pitied what he called culturally impoverished Africa and claimed that Indians, like Jews, are irrepressibly creative in spite of centuries of oppression.[22] In contrast with the "selfish, godless and hypocritical" civilization of the West, he claimed that in the ancient days of the Indian civilization "men were kind, God-fearing and simple and looked upon the body as a means of spiritual uplift."[23] While he recognized the dark side of the Indian tradition, he often used a rhetoric about the past that made it appear bathed in light.

As we have said, Gandhi's sojourn of twenty years among the Indians in South Africa introduced him to an all-Indian solidarity, beyond the differences in religion and caste. He acquired personal friends who were devout Muslims. In *Hind Swaraj* he wrote an entire chapter on Hindu-Muslim solidarity.[24] "India does not cease to be one nation," he wrote, "because people belonging to different religions live in it. The introduction of foreigners does not necessarily destroy the nation; they merge in it. The country must have a faculty of assimilation. India has always been such a country." The religions of India have been infused by Hindu sensitivities. To speak of an inborn enmity between Hindus and Muslims was a lie invented by their mutual enemy. Prior to the arrival of the British, Hindus and Muslims had learnt to live in peace. Gandhi was convinced that the world religions, when followed in accordance with their deepest meaning, actually converge and lead the believers to worship the divine and live a life of selfless service. In a statement issued in 1938, prior to a meeting with Jinnah, the leader of the Muslim League, Gandhi said: "My Hinduism is not sectarian. It includes all that I know to be best in Islam, Christianity, Buddhism, and Zoroastrianism. I am a life-long worker in the cause of Hindu-Muslim unity. It has been my passion from early youth."[25]

Another dimension of Gandhi's nationalism was the importance he attached to language.[26] The creation of a nation-state demands the ability of the citizens to converse with one another. Thanks to the British conquest, English had become the common language of the Indian elites. They were trained in English in the schools of India and at the universities of Britain, and they published their political ideas and carried on their debates in English. Some of the Extreme Nationalists did not want the language of the British empire to become the common tongue of the Indian people. Gandhi agreed with them. He believed that speaking English introduced Indians to the materialist civilization and weakened their religious sensibilities. He therefore fostered the strengthening of the Indian vernaculars. Ashamed that his native Gujarati had become rather rusty, he made an effort to repossess his own language. Could Hindi become the common Indian tongue, an idea supported by some nationalists? Gandhi favoured this idea when writing *Hind Swaraj*,[27] but later seems to have put more emphasis on India's linguistic pluralism. Since he regarded English as an instrument of Westernization, he did not want the Indian schools to accompany the teaching of the vernacular with an initiation into English. Teaching English in the schools, he argued, creates an elite class increasingly unable to express itself in its own vernacular while continuing to make all kind of mistakes in English. How can a broken language become the bond that unites a nation? In his book *Gandhi's Truth*, Eric Erikson recognizes the cultural and political consequences of the Indian situation where people were forced to communicate in a language they did not fully possess.

Truth becomes a hazy matter indeed when most official business and much of everyday life of a people must be transacted in a stilted and often broken English ... offering no more than an approximation of intended meaning. And since this fact, in the long run, makes it impossible and unnecessary to say what one "really" means, it supports a form of habitual half-truth such as the English had come to consider "inborn" in all Indians.[28]

Gandhi insisted that an educated Indian must know more than his or her own vernacular. He himself revived his own Gujarati, learnt Hindi and some Urdu, but made only little progress in Tamil and less in Telugu. Gandhi wished that he had studied Sanskrit from which Hindi and other Indian languages are derived. For Indians Sanskrit remains a source of inspiration. When Gandhi introduced concepts for which no terms existed in Gujarati, he used Sanskrit roots to create new words, such as *satya/graha* (truth-force) where *satya* is Sanskrit for truth and *agraha* for firmness. Because he looked forward to the creation of an independent Indian nation, he wanted Indians to be proud of their language. "To respect our own language, speak it well and use in it as few foreign words

as possible – this also is part of patriotism." "We must cultivate pride in our own language before we can speak proudly
of 'our country' with genuine feeling."[29]

THE DEBATE WITH TAGORE

The great Indian poet Rabindrath Tagore, whose writings were
widely read in Europe and America, was a religious humanist
and a passionate champion of justice and peace. He was
worried by World War I, the irrational, massive armed conflict
between the nations of Europe. Lecturing to American audi-
ences in 1917, he denounced nationalism as the great evil of
modern society. He distinguished between two antithetical
products of modernity, the "spirit of the West" and what he
called the "Nation of the West."[30]

India, Tagore told his audience, was exposed to both of
these products. The "spirit of the West" introduced India to
institutions that upheld a universal standard of justice for all,
irrespective of their caste and colour. The tyranny, injustice,
and extortion practiced at times by Indian princes were overcome by the rule of law set up by the British government,
creating order in this vast land inhabited by peoples of different races, languages, and customs. The spirit of the West, for
which Tagore was grateful, made it possible for these peoples
to enter into communication and strive to create a common
bond of friendship and cooperation. This happened, Tagore
added, in spite of the "Nation of the West."

The "Nation of the West" is the concentration of power
in the government, aimed at conquest and total control. Over
the centuries India has experienced oppression from princes
and foreign powers, but this was mild compared with the
oppression brought by the British, the Western Nation. The
difference between the two forms of government resembles
that between the hand-loom and the power-loom, the latter

being inanimate, relentless, accurate, and predictable. The Nation sees to it that our people suffer humiliation. We find ourselves deprived of an appropriate education and at the same time jeered by the Nation for lagging behind. We are excluded from any governmental responsibility for our country, and at the same time despised by the Nation for the lack of experience in governing ourselves. Such is the hypocrisy and the cynicism of the Nation that it presents itself as taking upon itself the white man's burden of civilizing the East.

The truth is, Tagore continued, that the spirit of conflict and conquest is at the origin and in the centre of Western nationalism. In the Great War the nations revealed their true nature: they are like a pack of predatory creatures who must have their victims and destroy one another. The Nation of the West is the massive obstacle to spreading the spirit of the West, the spirit that recognizes a universal moral law and fosters the pacification of humankind in justice, cooperation, and shared responsibility. If the Nation races ahead, unchecked by moral considerations, it will become increasingly blind, irrational and obsessed, and end up by destroying itself.

Tagore here refers to a paradox of modernity that was clearly recognized by social thinkers in the nineteenth century. The struggle against the feudal order and the creation of the democratic state represented the modern idea of responsible citizenship and universal justice and, at the same time, invested the government with the powers previously distributed among different princely dynasties and regional and local communities. The conservative critics of the Enlightenment saw very clearly that the liberal nationalist movements which created the modern nation-state produced, despite ideals of liberty, equality, and solidarity, an intense controlling power reaching into every corner of society, the likes of which had not existed in previous ages.[31] Traditional tyranny, while oppressive and hateful, was arbitrary and limited in its outreach, possessing neither a scientifically schooled state bureaucracy nor the legislative instruments for making universal laws. Social thinkers who approved of the democratic revolution also recognized the danger of total control, but they believed that society's political, social, and economic institutions would be able to limit and direct the power of the state. Yet they did not deny the paradox that the liberal state was both the mediator of democratic values and an instrument of new and previously unheard-of power. Reading Tagore, one has the impression that he naively believed the spirit of the West and the Nation of the West could be separated.

In 1921, when Gandhi started his first great non-cooperation campaign, Tagore was giving lectures in Europe. He was delighted by the letters he received reporting on the political development in India. In a letter to a friend he praised Gandhi. In fact, Tagore venerated Gandhi: it was he who gave Gandhi the title *Mahatma* (great soul).[32] The following paragraph reveals Tagore's admiration for Gandhi as he looked at him from distant Europe.

The truth that moral force is a higher power than brute force will be proved by the people who are unarmed ... The day is sure to come when the frail man of the spirit, completely unhampered by airfleets and dreadnoughts, will prove that the meek are to inherit the earth. It is in the fittingness of things that Mahatma Gandhi, frail in body and devoid of all material resources, should call up the immense power of the meek that has been waiting in the heart of the destitute and insulted humanity of India. The destiny of India has chosen as its ally the power of soul, and not that of muscle. And she is to raise the history of man from the muddy level of physical conflict to the higher moral attitude.[33]

Yet when Tagore returned to India in the same year, he was deeply disturbed by what he regarded as a fanatical element in Gandhi's nation-wide campaign to refuse English education, burn British-made cloth, and urge people of all classes to "spin and weave" and make their own, homespun clothes. Tagore's internationalism clashed with Gandhi's nationalism. After a private meeting of the two, in which they were unable to resolve their disagreement, Tagore decided with a heavy heart to publish "The Call of Truth," an essay directed against the man whom he greatly admired. "The Mahatma," he writes, "has won the heart of India with his love; for that we have all acknowledged his sovereignty. He has given us a vision of the *shakti* (divine creative power) of truth; for that our gratitude to him is unbounded." With him we desire Indian self-government grounded in the *swaraj* of each person. But against him we must now oppose his narrow nationalist campaign marked by the slogan "Spin and weave."[34]

The reasons Tagore gives are not very clear. If I understand him correctly, he seems to share Gandhi's political aim of having India become a sovereign, independent nation. In his essay, I notice, Tagore does not warn the Indian people, following his previous political analysis, that an Indian nation-state would be drawn into the oppressive and aggressive games played by the Nation of the West. Why, then, does Tagore oppose Gandhi's campaign? What seems especially distasteful to Tagore is Gandhi's appeal to all Indians to adopt the lifestyle of peasants. He depicts Gandhi's program as narrow, focusing on material instead of spiritual issues and reflecting resentment rather than wisdom. When Gandhi, Tagore writes, declared war against the tyranny of the machine which is oppressing the whole world, we all enrolled under his banner. But we must oppose his present campaign because it tries to replace one slavery by another.

Tagore sees a new spirit at work in the world, the spirit of the West now on a global scale, favouring the self-determination of the nations still under imperial or colonial control. He praises the League of Nations committed to universal justice, English politicians who support home rule for India, and the new internationalism among the young people of Europe. Gandhi, he thinks, misjudges the present historical situation. We need friends in the world, not enemies. Should we go on complaining, he asks, refusing to cooperate, harping on the faults of other nations and striving for *swaraj* on the foundation of quarrelsomeness? If we learn to think in terms of international solidarity, we shall arrive at home rule on a road without conflicts. "From now on," Tagore writes, "any nation which takes an isolated view of its own country will run counter the spirit of the New Age and know no peace. From now on, the anxiety each country has for its own safety must embrace the welfare of the world."[35] Gandhi's nationalism isolates us, and will have destructive consequences.

Tagore's attack did not go unanswered. Gandhi gave a passionate reply to his friend, the Poet, in which he explains in the most radical terms the spiritual meaning of his campaign:

To a people famished and idle, the only acceptable form in which God can dare appear is work and the promise of food for wages. God created man to work for his food, and that those who are without work were thieves. … Hunger is the argument that is driving India to the spinning wheel. The call of the spinning wheel is the noblest of all. Because it is a call of love. And love is *swaraj*.[36]

Spinning and weaving will employ the masses presently trapped in idleness and despair. But what about the well-to-do? Why, Gandhi asks, should those who have no need to work for food, spin? He replies: because they are now eating what does not belong to them. I am living, he adds, on the spoliation of my countrymen. We must all work with our hands. "I claim that in losing the spinning wheel we lost our left lung: we are, therefore, suffering from galloping consumption.

The restoration of the wheel arrests the progress of the fell disease."[37] In this period of transition, all Indians must turn to the spinning wheel, which for the vast majority of them will remain a necessary occupation for all times.

We have lost the spinning wheel, Gandhi continues, because of our love of foreign cloth. "Therefore I consider it a sin to wear foreign cloth." Gandhi tells his readers that he draws no sharp distinction between economics and ethics. Economic activities that hurt the moral well-being of an individual or a nation are immoral and therefore sinful. It is sinful to buy and use articles made by sweated labour. It is sinful to import goods from overseas if by doing so we leave our own people unemployed and condemn them to starvation. That is the reason, Gandhi explains, why he has burnt his foreign clothes as a ritual of purification, and he urges his Indian countrymen to follow his example and be content with rough, homespun cloth produced in their neighbourhood. "In burning my foreign clothes I burn my shame." I will not give these clothes to the poor who have no cover: "I refuse to insult the naked by giving them clothes they do not need, instead of giving them work which they sorely need."[38] The Poet is, therefore, wrong when he thinks the campaign of spinning and weaving is preoccupied with material instead of spiritual issues.

Is Tagore right when he accuses Gandhi's nationalism of being devoid of universal solidarity? Gandhi replies that the message of non-violence and non-cooperation is not isolating Indians from humanity but making them teachers offering practical wisdom applicable to the struggle for justice in many parts of the world. What else, he asks, do we have to offer to the world? If we try to export our sacred scriptures, the powerful of the world, irreligious as they are, will not believe our message because we, the heirs and custodians of the ancient wisdom, do not now live by them. We are in need of conversion. Our non-cooperation does not exclude the peoples of the world; it offers resistance to an evil system that oppresses us and oppresses others. We bear no hostility toward the English. We want them to be rescued from their material civilization and its attendant greed and exploitation of the weak. "Come and cooperate with us on our terms, and it will be well for us, for you and the world." On another occasion Gandhi writes, "India's task must be to convert the rest of the world, including the British, to her ancient life-style and to save mankind from becoming still further enmeshed in the tools of overmechanized and underspiritualized civilization emanating from Europe."[39]

Like Martin Buber, Gandhi insists that nationalism is not at odds with internationalism. The struggle for national self-determination for the sake of the poor and in the name of truth and justice is a universal principle promoting the pacification of humankind. "Indian nationalism," Gandhi writes, "is not exclusive, nor aggressive, nor destructive. It is health-giving, religious, and therefore humanitarian."[40]

In his attack on Gandhi, we noted above, Tagore did not mention the problem he had previously raised, that by becoming a modern nation India would imitate the Nation of the West and find itself at odds with the Western spirit of the rule of law and universal justice. Since Tagore did not bring up this issue, Gandhi does not discuss it in his reply. He did not have to be reminded by Tagore that the modern state is a dangerous institution. Gandhi had anarchist sympathies. "The state," he writes, "represents violence in a concentrated and organized form. The individual has a soul, but the state is a soulless machine, it cannot be weaned from violence to which it owes its existence."[41] Still, Gandhi wanted an Indian state. He hoped that its power could be restrained. "The best government is one that governs least," he wrote. He recommended "loyalty to the state, yes, but first to conscience."

What Gandhi did not discuss, or did not fully recognize, was that nationalism, the cultural and political movement to create a sovereign nation-state, is a modernizing social phenomenon. While he claimed that Indians had nothing to learn from the West, his wish to liberate the Indian people from British colonial power, overcome the feudal rule of the Indian princes, and create a cooperative and egalitarian society was generated by his contact with the aspirations of Western Enlightenment. Gandhi's social movement, if successful, would necessarily create a modern state, imitating Western models. To create a society that respects the dignity of its citizens, rescues the poor from their exclusion, ensures people's equality before the law, and overcomes the hierarchical discrimination inherited from the past demands the establishment of a supreme controlling institution, the modern state, with the power to impose and protect the just and humanely conceived social order. Gandhi hoped, one supposes, that some form of democracy, not yet invented, would assure subsidiarity and decentralization.

4
Paul Tillich's
Ethic of Nationalism

After moving to the United States in 1933, Paul Tillich became one of the most famous Protestant theologians of the twentieth century. In Germany, as a young man from a conservative family, he had been so deeply shaken by World War I that he became an ardent socialist in active solidarity with the working class. He founded a circle of religious socialists, including Christians and Jews, and edited a review promoting the cause of socialist justice.[1] When, in the early thirties, the Nazi Party received increasing support from the population, Tillich gave a series of public lectures in which he engaged Germans in conversation about politics and ethics. These lectures became a book, *The Socialist Decision*,[2] which offered a systematic treatment from a Christian point of view of the political ideologies present in Germany, in particular the relationship of socialism and nationalism. The book was published in January 1933, just as Hitler was coming into power. Since Tillich had written in his preface that National-Socialism "not only negates socialism but in fact threatens the future of the nation and of Western civilization,"[3] the book could no longer be distributed. It was never reviewed in a scholarly journal. When the book was officially condemned, most of the copies were destroyed. Later in the same year, Tillich himself had to flee Nazi Germany and sought refuge in the United States of America.

Tillich was one of the few anti-fascist writers of the thirties who did not oppose nationalism on principle. He had respect for people united by the same origin or the same culture who were struggling to protect their community and their land from the social forces that undermined them. Since Tillich recognized that struggles of this kind easily generate injustices, he distinguished between ethically acceptable and ethically unacceptable forms of nationalism. He offered his ethical reflections as part of a systematic anthropological and theological analysis of political parties and ideologies. Although *The Socialist Decision* is a groundbreaking study in political science, political scientists have paid almost no attention to it, one reason being that the book almost disappeared after its publication in German, and the English translation came out only in 1977. Another reason is, I think, that in this book Tillich, as a socialist, offers a constructive critique of socialism that questions several Marxist assumptions. Tillich argues that socialism can become sound and faithful to its own inspiration only if it is willing to respect and build upon people's cultural, ethnic, and religious roots. In this chapter I shall present an analysis of Tillich's book and articulate the ethics of nationalism contained in it.

It is worth mentioning that the political economist Karl Polanyi was another anti-fascist thinker of the thirties who honoured people's struggle to protect their community, culture, and land against the social forces that undermined them. Polanyi recognized that neither liberals nor Marxists had a correct understanding of the social nature of human existence. Economic liberals believed that people always acted to advance their rational self-interest, while Marxists held that people acted, consciously or unconsciously, to promote the material interest of their class. These ideologies overlooked people's rootedness in community and tradition. Polanyi spoke of fascism as "the return of the repressed," the return to the roots of the national community, but now in distorted form, demanding that people sacrifice their personal conscience in obedience to the collectivity.[4]

Paul Tillich begins his book with a philosophical reflection. He holds that people's political sympathies are responses to the human condition as such. But what is the human condition? Influenced by the existentialism of the young Heidegger, Tillich holds that as human beings we experience ourselves as thrown into the world, as homeless and futureless, deeply disturbed by our lack of orientation and challenged by two troubling questions: Where do we come from? and What is our future? This, according to Tillich, is the human condition. It compels people to question themselves in regard to the "whence" and the "whither" of their social existence.

THE POWERS OF ORIGIN

Let us first look at the people who are haunted by the "whence" question. People asking this first question look back to their origins, treasure the memories of the past, and protect the values cherished by their community from the beginning. They become deeply attached to their roots. In Tillich's terminology, their political imagination is determined by a "myth of origin" and their political orientation deserves the name of "political romanticism." Political romanticism exists in a "conservative form," found in the European political parties that sought to protect feudal values and the feudal elites and resisted the impact of capitalism and democracy. Yet political romanticism also exists in a "revolutionary form," present in European fascism, in particular the German National-Socialist Party. Tillich here refers to the anti-bourgeois rhetoric adopted by European fascists, including the Nazis, their promise to overthrow the traditional elites, their rejection of democracy, human rights, and international capitalism, and their effort to revive the long-forgotten values of the people's distant past, in the German case pre-Christian pagan mythology. Tillich is fully aware that in the thirties, opposition to the economic establishment was no longer emphasized by the Nazi Party. He mentions specifically that the Führer, hoping to win the support of the German economic elite, presented the Nazi movement as a protection for German capital against the communist threat. Still, prior to 1933 many members of the Nazi movement were committed to revolutionary political romanticism.

When Tillich speaks of "myths," following the usage of social scientists, he is referring not to fictions or false beliefs, but to what people hold to be self-evident, their beliefs and their values. Thus the myths of origin are many, some based on soil, blood, religion, community, or nationhood. Some stories and memories of origin combine several or even all these roots. Tillich believes that the myths of origin create solidarity, generate social power, and enable people to engage in joint political action. These myths, Tillich argues, generate "eros" and "fate." By eros, he means an emotional attachment to family, tribe, soil, or community, rooted in memories of childhood, an attachment that renders people capable of disregarding their personal advantage and serving the common cause. And by fate, Tillich means the overwhelming sense that the community into which individuals are born has a significant past and a particular destiny which they cannot evade, which demands their loyalty, and which, therefore, creates a strong communal bond. Eros and fate thus understood empower a people to transcend modern individualism and utilitarianism, serve the common good of their society, and possibly even create new forms of social existence beyond human alienation.

We have found a similar argument in Martin Buber's speeches on Judaism. Buber tried to persuade assimilated, liberal

Jews and old-fashioned, orthodox Jews that by embracing religious Zionism as a new form of Jewish existence, based on memory and destiny, the liberals would be rescued from their rootlessness and the orthodox from their otherworldiness. The return to roots and the sense of a common fate, Buber held, are the foundation for a strong national community.

This idea is shared by many thinkers conscious of the social substance of human life. Thus the American Protestant theologian H. Richard Niebuhr writes,

Where common memory is lacking, where (humans) do not share the same past, there can be no real community, and where community is to be formed common memory must be created. ... The measure of our distance from each other in our nations and our groups can be taken by noting the divergence, the separateness and the lack of sympathy in our social memories. Conversely, the measure of our unity is the extent of our common memory.[5]

After World War I, we recall, Martin Buber recognized the ambiguity of the quest for roots, national identity, and political self-determination, realizing the crimes that this quest had so often generated. He began to emphasize in the strongest terms that the Zionist movement must remain subject to the ethical norms of Prophetic Judaism.[6] We shall find a similar emphasis in Tillich arguing that any politics of rootedness is dangerous unless subjected to strict ethical norms. In the twenties, it is worth noting, Buber was an active member of Tillich's circle of religious socialists.

According to Tillich, political romanticism, or the political orientation guided by a myth of origin, is caught in a tragic contradiction. On the one hand, political romanticism is optimistic: political conservatives believe in social harmony and look forward to the creation of organic unity and ideological consensus in society. Since conservatives trust the powers of origin, the social bond uniting the people and their dedication to the common good, they – the conservatives – believe that society will be able to transcend its internal conflicts and achieve unanimity of thought and purpose. On the other hand, the myth of origin inevitably creates a division in humanity between "us" and "them," insiders and outsiders, brothers and enemies. The same myth, moreover, tends to create a division within the community of origin between "higher" and "lower," chiefs and followers, princes and subjects – and, we would add, men and women. To make the myth of origin the sole guide of a society's political orientation will therefore generate hostility to outsiders and lead to war, and within the society itself, produce inequality, injustice, and eventually oppression. This, then, is the baneful contradiction of political romanticism: it praises unity and actually creates division.

At this point, Tillich, the theologian, adds that the classical Hebrew prophecy recorded in the Bible broke the myth of origin which until then had largely shaped the religion of the covenanted people. The unconditional demand (*Forderung*) announced by the prophets was the practice of social justice. Without commitment to social justice, being a member of the chosen people or even its anointed king meant nothing in God's eyes. Since, according to the prophets, the God of Israel was eternally intolerant of oppression, fidelity to the divine covenant meant above all showing justice and mercy to the poor, the stranger, the weak, and the vulnerable.

Tillich agrees with several social thinkers, amongst them Ernst Bloch and Karl Mannheim,[7] who relate the emergence of the secular, radical tradition in Western society to the restless yearning for a just, egalitarian society in Hebrew prophecy, mediated in the West by heterodox Christian sectarian movements. At the same time, Tillich continues, while the prophets broke the myth of origin, they did not declare it irrelevant or devoid of significance. On the contrary, the prophets held that the unconditional demand of justice revealed the deepest meaning of the ancient covenant and hence created a new and higher bond with the community of origin, celebrating the solidarity and the destiny inscribed in its foundation.

THE UNCONDITIONAL DEMAND

Let us now turn to the people who are haunted by the "whither" question. The anxiety generated by the human condition urges them to ask what is expected of them and where are they going. The memories and stories that fill their imagination are myths of challenges and obligations. Tillich calls them "myths of demand." The word "demand" is the not quite accurate translation of the German *Forderung*, which suggests challenge, summons, and obligation. People haunted by such myths have a strong sense that what "is" is not what it "ought" to be. They hold that the "is" must never be separated from the "ought"; and since historical reality is never what it should be, they yearn for its transformation. They are, therefore, critical of the world in which they live and try to change it. These people are forever restless; they feel addressed by an ethical summons and obliged to act in accordance with a higher demand.

The prophetic principle in the Bible, to which reference has been made above, is an example of such a myth of demand. Here the demand is unconditional since it is of divine origin. In modern times, the myths of demand are expressed in secular terms and, according to Tillich, generate corresponding political orientations, first the Enlightenment protest of the bourgeoisie against the feudal order and later the socialist protest against bourgeois society.

Enlightenment and bourgeois revolution, Tillich argues, was inspired by the overriding idea – he calls it the "bourgeois principle" – that universal reason was the instrument of human liberation. The universality of reason, it was then believed, was able to dissolve the irrational bonds of family, tribe, church, and community that bound people to the feudal-aristocratic order. Enlightenment reason was thus suspicious of the powers of origin. Reason severed people from their feelings, their attachments, and their prejudices and rescued them from their identification with a particular tradition created by a myth of origin.

The bourgeois principle, Tillich continues, is embodied in two different forms existing in a certain tension with one another. The first of these is "the liberal principle." It affirms personal freedom, especially economic freedom, against the strict controls of mercantilism imposed by the absolute monarchy. Liberalism looks upon the human being as a rational agent bent on self-preservation and the enhancement of his material well-being. Universal reason here demands that individuals recognize that they are responsible for their own lives and obliged to promote their material interests in competition with their neighbour. The rational life allows people to escape from the virtues forced upon them by traditional culture and religion. Since the free market economy corresponds to the demand of reason, liberalism undermines people's traditional economic activities, embedded as they were in their social existence and inspired not by the desire for profit but by a social motivation as members of a community. Tillich alludes here to a theme later to be explored in detail by Karl Polanyi.[8]

At the same time, Tillich continues, despite its emphasis on competition, liberalism believes in harmony. Liberals hold the optimistic position that universal reason steers humanity toward emancipation. According to capitalist theory, the market mechanism – as by a hidden hand – transforms the unmitigated self-interest of the players into a coordinated economic activity serving the material well-being of society as a whole. Tillich calls this believing in miracles.

The other form of the bourgeois idea is "the democratic principle." It calls for a rational society transcending the inequalities, prejudices, and arbitrariness of the feudal-aristocratic order. Democratic theory looks upon human beings as rational agents co-responsible for the society to which they belong. Reason demands that people create a society of equals, produce a constitution that establishes freedom and justice, and invest the government with the power to protect and promote the requirements of reason, i.e. the well-being of society as a whole. The democratic principle implies that government has a certain responsibility for the nation's economic well-being, an idea – as we noted above – at odds with the liberal principle. Rational democracy and capitalist economy exist in tension with one another.

While the democratic principle intends to deliver people from the inherited bonds of family, clan, tribe, and community, it demands the creation of the nation-state and hence calls forth a spirit of nationalism. This rational nationalism is meant to overcome the sentimental ties that bind people to their traditional communities in the old order. Still, when it suits their rational purpose, for instance to protect the unity of the nation or prepare for war, bourgeois democrats willingly invoke certain myths of origin and draw upon the collective sentiment of particular sectors of the population. And, Tillich continues, when threatened by working-class movements or other forms of social unrest, these democrats are often ready to ally themselves with the remnant of the feudal elites and invoke the symbols of political romanticism.

In its own way, the democratic principle presupposes harmony. It is confident that thanks to the universality of reason, the various sectors and classes in society will be able, despite their different material interests, to achieve political consensus. While there exists a certain tension between the liberal and the democratic principle, they both embody typical bourgeois optimism.

The bourgeois principle in its liberal and democratic form is an expression of rationalism which, in the course of the nineteenth century, became more and more techno-scientific, i.e. increasingly identified with instrumental reason. In his critique of bourgeois society, Tillich follows what we, in the previous chapters, have called the Weberian critique of modernity, especially as it was developed by Marxist thinker Georg Lukacs and philosophers Max Horkheimer and Theodor Adorno of the Frankfurt School of Social Research, with whom Tillich was well acquainted.[9] Lukacs had accused the modern, techno-rational society of "reifying" human life and thereby causing the death of the human spirit, a critique that was accepted by the Frankfurt School.

According to Tillich, then, scientific rationalism produces the "reification" of human existence. According to liberalism, personal life is fully determined because people are by nature utility maximizers and hence their behaviour can be calculated scientifically. Even in democratic theory, the rational policies adopted by government are less and less derived from a public debate involving different sectors of society, but are in growing measure derived from social scientific studies commissioned by government and executed in the spirit of positivism. In liberalism and democratic theory, people are increasingly looked upon as objects or things that move according to scientifically determined laws and can thus be controlled and manipulated.

The reification inflicted upon people by bourgeois society separates them from the wellsprings and forces of life – an idea shared, as we saw, by Buber and Gandhi. Universal reason estranges people from their emotions, their imagination, their bodies, their community, and the profound aspirations that transcend their material concerns. People here become severed from the powers of origin. This, according to Tillich, is the internal contradiction of bourgeois Enlightenment: it promises to liberate people for human life, yet actually cuts them off from the sources of human life.

No wonder, Tillich continues, so many people turn to political romanticism in its conservative or even its revolutionary or fascist form. By returning to a myth of origin, people hope to find community, gain access to imagination and emotions, and re-appropriate their bodies so that they are no longer defined as an instrument of production. Yet, as we saw above, political romanticism itself suffers from an internal contradiction: it promises the organic unity of society, yet actually produces inequality, injustice, and eventually oppression.

Here is a summary of Tillich's categories:

political romanticism – a myth of origin	{	conservatism, nostalgia for the *ancien régime* fascist revolution, violent return primitive roots
the bourgeois principle, – a myth of demand	{	economic principle, liberalism, trust in the market democratic principle, liberalism, trust in the state

Both political romanticism and the bourgeois project suffer from internal contradiction and, despite their optimism, generate oppression and alienation.

CAN SOCIALISM RESOLVE THESE CONTRADICTIONS?

Tillich, the philosopher, holds that the two questions of "whence" and "whither," generated by human existence itself, belong together and should never be separated. Being totally preoccupied with one question and forgetting about the other (as exemplified in political romanticism and bourgeois Enlightenment) inevitably leads to one-sidedness and distortion with unsettling and even dangerous political consequences. Tillich, the theologian, insists – as we saw above – that the divine summons uttered in the prophetic tradition of the Bible broke the myth of origin, subjected it to the unconditional norm of justice, and in doing so fulfilled the myth of origin in a new and unexpected way. Here the myth of demand was not proposed from outside of the powers of origin, but as a hidden yearning inscribed in the myth of origin from the beginning.

Tillich now raises the question whether socialism is able to resolve the contradictions of political romanticism and bourgeois Enlightenment. His answer to this question is complex; it demands a lengthy explanation. I shall first mention Tillich's bold and original proposal, and then explain its meaning and present the arguments which he offered for it. The proposal is that *if existing socialism underwent a conversion to its true nature and guiding principle, it would be able to draw upon the powers of origin in its struggle to realize the unconditional demand of justice and initiate a more humane, qualitatively different society.*

The existing forms of socialism will not do. Tillich refers especially to the communist regime in the Soviet Union and the social democratic and communist parties in the West. These forms of socialism, he argues, are involved in a contradiction, because they try to overcome the bourgeois principle while actually remaining dependent on it. What this puzzling sentence means I shall explain in the following paragraphs.

Socialism rejected the bourgeois principle, first, by repudiating the bourgeois faith in harmony. Socialists did not share the historical optimism that universal reason was guiding humanity in a peaceful evolution toward happiness. Socialists were convinced that class oppression in bourgeois society, as in all previous societies, brought forth not evolution but division, oppression, and revolution. They interpreted the interplay of forces in capitalist society not as a democratic search for social consensus but as a conflict between the capitalist class and the proletariat. Tillich fully accepted this socialist analysis. In the thirties, he too regarded the working class as the historical agent of revolution, destined to remake industrial society in a more just and more egalitarian form.

Socialism rejected, secondly, the liberal form of the bourgeois principle: individualism, competitiveness, capitalism, the maximization of personal freedom, and the naive faith in the guidance of the hidden hand. Against liberalism, socialism stood for solidarity, cooperation, egalitarianism, economic planning, and an ethos of personal sacrifice for the sake of the good cause.

Yet socialism, Tillich argues, has embraced the democratic form of the bourgeois principle by interpreting it in a more radical way. Enlightenment reason provided socialism with the myth of demand, that is to say the unconditional summons to economic justice. Socialists were convinced that society was destined to become fully rational: they believed in social equality, democratic participation, and the duty of the government to protect citizens from exploitation and promote their economic well-being. Socialists believed in rational planning. They radicalized the democratic principle, interpreting it against the liberal principle.

Tillich is now able to argue that socialism has not totally freed itself from bourgeois Enlightenment. By endorsing the democratic principle, it shares the Enlightenment faith in the universality of reason. Socialism is incapable of understanding the particular, except as a concrete instance of the universal. Socialism encourages uncritical confidence in the natural and social sciences, remains indifferent to the non-rational dimension of human existence, undermines traditional values and the powers of origin, and embraces the same sort of historical determinism that makes people believe that scientists are able to predict the future.

While the existing socialisms pretend that they have overcome and left behind the bourgeois principle, they continue to be caught in it and despite their strenuous efforts are unable to move beyond it. Committed to universal reason and, like the bourgeoisie, dissolving all powers of origin – family, tribe, community, religion, and nation – socialism produces the same sort of "reification" that Georg Lukacs and other critical thinkers have attributed to bourgeois society. Against its own intention, socialism squeezes the vital forces of human nature into narrow behavioural patterns that can be grasped scientifically and controlled by rational planning. Despite its utopian vision, socialism tends to cripple the imagination and dampen the human spirit.

The reifying impact of socialism, Tillich argues, is the reason why much of the opposition against socialism is not based on the defense of capitalism, but rather on the protest of people against a political orientation that does not respect their non-rational roots in the place or the community to which they belong. For the sake of economic advantage, a wide range of people other than industrial workers might turn to socialism: farmers, artisans, low-level clerks and officials, and poor people in the country and small towns. But these people tend to reject socialism, largely for cultural reasons, the protection of their roots. Labelling this attitude "false consciousness" only reveals the commitment of the existing socialism to a barren, scientific rationalism of bourgeois origin.

SOCIALISM AND THE POWER OF ORIGINS

Tillich does not believe that socialism is forever caught in the net of the bourgeois Enlightenment. The original contribution to political thought made in Tillich's *The Socialist Decision* is his careful analysis of the "socialist principle." By "principle" Tillich means the overriding idea that guides a social movement, embodies the movement's original inspiration, and operates as a corrective of inauthentic or false developments. In this sense, Tillich spoke of the bourgeois principle. But what is, according to him, the socialist principle? It should not be identified with the radicalization of the democratic form of bourgeois Enlightenment, as socialists usually do. While the Enlightenment heritage is precious, providing socialism with a myth of demand, it needs a cultural counterweight, derived from a myth of origin, to rescue it from the trend toward reification.

But does socialism have roots in the powers of origin? Mainstream socialist thinkers tend to deny this. For them socialism is inspired by the material self-interest of the working class and the emancipatory thrust of scientific reason.

Tillich disagrees with this. His *first* argument is not new to us. We alluded to it above. With many historical scholars Tillich holds that the utopian vision of socialism, a society transcending the exploitation of humans by humans, is much older than the Enlightenment, that it originated in classical Hebrew prophecy and was mediated to the modern age by Jewish and Christian religious currents. The Marxist philosopher Ernst Bloch, in his 1918 book, *Geist der Utopie*, documented the biblical origin of the socialist utopia, and the liberal sociologist Karl Mannheim presented a similar analysis in his book *Ideology and Utopia*, published in 1928. It is true, Tillich adds, that mainstream religion has always allied itself with the existing secular powers and hence represented a conservative force. Still, socialism made and makes a serious mistake, Tillich argues, by its refusal to recognize the counter-current of radical religion. In Marxist theory, religion was simply identified with ideology. When the German Social Democratic

Party in the Erfurt Programme of 1891 decided to become more generous to its believing Christian members, it defined religion as a purely private affair, to which the Party had no objection. In doing so, German socialism followed the bourgeois idea of religion as a private, spiritual journey, unrelated to society. Socialism failed to recognize the radical potential of biblical religion and hence its own rootedness in a myth of origin.

Tillich's *second* argument is original. He sees a contradiction in the socialist understanding of the working class. On the one hand, socialists depict the proletariat as exploited, oppressed, and alienated from their humanity. Workers have become pawns in the capitalist system, they are treated as commodities, and they have been made to think of themselves as objects, not as subjects, of production. On the other hand, this same working class, this victim of capitalist dehumanization, is presented as the historical agent of world revolution, through whose political struggle the whole of humanity will experience liberation. In socialist theory, the proletariat is dehumanized and yet humanizing: it is weak and wounded, and yet strong and healthy. Tillich regards this as a contradiction.

He argues, by contrast, that the description of working people as alienated and dehumanized has been greatly exaggerated. Their struggle against the capitalist system is never based simply on the material self-interest of their economic class, but also and especially on the longing to protect their humanity and their communal roots against the destructive inroads of the industrial economy and its driving spirit. Their resistance to capitalism is not simply economic, Tillich argues, but cultural. The conventional socialist analysis does not take seriously that workers have wives and children, are attached to their families, have a special love of their region, and are heirs of a local culture. Socialist theory does not understand the true nature of working-class solidarity. If solidarity is simply defined as loyalty in a struggle against a common enemy, it would evaporate once the enemy is gone. A solidarity that lasts has deeper roots: it is based on love, on community, on an identification with an ethical tradition. Because workers are still rooted people, because they still cherish a myth of origin, because love and sacrifice still mean something to them, they recognize the destructive force of the capitalist economy and have the will and the power to organize a revolutionary movement of resistance and reconstruction.

What follows from this is that the socialist principle incarnates two trends in tension with one another, the emancipatory reason of the Enlightenment (a myth of demand) and rootedness in the powers of human life (a myth of origin). Here the unconditional demand of justice is not external to the powers of origin, but expresses the hidden longing inscribed in these powers from the beginning. If socialism wants to be faithful to the socialist principle, Tillich argues, it is in need of conversion. In explaining the title of his book, Tillich says that the call for "the socialist decision" is addressed not only to non-socialists but also and especially to socialists themselves. To transcend bourgeois rationalism and overcome the massive trend toward reification, socialism must allow itself to be corrected by the socialist principle. Without abandoning the unconditional demand of justice, socialism must lay hold of its own myth of origin and gain access to the forces of life: imagination, passion, and community. Then socialism will stop undermining the myths of origin and cease to alienate a wide section of the population that would have economic reasons for becoming socialists.

Tillich offered a *third* argument that the socialist principle transcended Enlightenment rationalism. According to the bourgeois principle in its liberal and democratic forms, universal reason is incarnate in history, human behaviour follows a set of recognizable laws, and concrete historical developments can be understood scientifically. Hence it is possible to predict the future. In other words, the future is totally contained in causes available in the present. There are no real surprises in history: the future is simply an extrapolation of the present situation. In the perspective of Enlightenment reason, this was good news. Why? Because Enlightenment optimism supposed that reason operative in society was moving it toward social harmony.

Socialists did not share this optimism. They believed that reason exacerbated conflict in society and led to revolution. Still, they shared with bourgeois Enlightenment the trust in the scientific interpretation of history and therefore believed that scientists who followed a socialist perspective could predict the future. For socialists too, the future was an extrapolation of the present.

Tillich discerns a contradiction in this scientific belief. On the one hand, socialists wanted the working class to gain power, overcome the dictatorship of the bourgeoisie, and establish a new, classless society ruled, for a time, by working-class dictatorship. On the other hand, socialists denounced domination, wished to be liberated from the power of the state, and expected the dictatorship of the proletariat to be a brief episode. Socialists thought that power could be used to liberate the world from power and that violence could be employed to banish violence from the earth.

Tillich thinks that such a belief is irrational. Yet the grain of truth in this irrational belief, Tillich continues, deserves attention. The paradoxical position reveals that socialists, despite their theory, do not really accept the scientific predictability of history. They do not really believe that the future is fully contained in the causes given in the present; in other words, they are open to "the new" in history. Socialists acknowledge, despite their theory, the surprising creativity of humans capable of transcending the behavioural patterns determined by their situation. While Tillich does not believe for a moment that it is possible to overcome power by power or violence by violence, he interpreted this socialist belief as a sign that the socialist principle transcended the rationalism of bourgeois Enlightenment and acknowledged the indeterminate nature of history and thus its openness to the unexpected.

Tillich calls this non-rational attitude toward the future "expectancy." As a theologian he is keenly aware that expectancy characterized the biblical attitude to history. The Bible saw history as the locus of the *mirabilia Dei*, the marvellous things God has done for the rescue of humanity from self-destruction. Believing Jews and Christians continue to believe that the future is open to God's unexpected and unmerited grace. Because of this biblical expectancy, theologians reject all Enlightenment theories of necessary evolution or historical determinism.

Among social scientists "expectancy" is rarely acknowledged. An important exception is Max Weber who rejected any form of historical determinism and acknowledged the possibility of the new and surprising. The theoretical basis for this attitude was Weber's concept of charismatic power. He argued that there were people gifted with a sudden charisma that enabled them to create a massive following and make people feel, think, and act in new ways, at odds with their tradition and contradicting the rationality of their society. Weber regarded charisma as a value-free concept applying to healers of humans as well as their destroyers.

But from where did the socialist principle derive its sense of expectancy? Tillich regards socialist expectancy as an inheritance from a myth of origin, the biblical utopia that, though unacknowledged, has nourished the socialist vision from the beginning. Tillich realized of course how dangerous it was in the early thirties to speak of "the new" or "the new age," for this vocabulary was adopted by Hitler and his National-Socialists.

The Nazis even cited Max Weber's social theory which assigned charisma an important role in the evolution of history. Yet Tillich did not hesitate to invoke symbols of origin and the non-rational expectation of the new, because he subordinated these powers to the unconditional demand of justice, proper to the socialist principle.

For these three reasons then, Tillich concludes that the socialist principle, while an heir of democratic Enlightenment and thus guided by a myth of demand, embodies at the same time certain myths of origin: i) a utopia inherited from ancient biblical longing and ii) the human values and future dreams of the community in which working people are still rooted. In his book he tries to show in detail how the conversion to the powers of origin would affect socialist theory and practice, widen its appeal beyond the proletariat and rescue the socialist parties from their internal contradictions.

The socialist principle, Tillich argues, is authentically grounded in human reality: it reflects the human wrestling with the two socio-existential questions, "whence?" and "whither?," and thus overcomes the one-sidedness and distortion of the bourgeois principle and of political romanticism.

This is a summary of Tillich's argument:

existing socialism
$\left\{\begin{array}{l}\text{rejects bourgeois evolutionary optimism} \\ \text{rejects bourgeois individualism} \\ \text{yet retains bourgeois rationalism} \\ \quad \text{cutting people off from their roots}\end{array}\right.$

socialism converted
to the socialist
principle
$\left\{\begin{array}{l}\text{retains "the myth of demand" contained} \\ \quad \text{in bourgeois rationalism} \\ \text{yet recognizes "the myth of origin"} \\ \quad \text{implicit in the socialist principle:} \\ \quad \text{its own social utopia and its passion} \\ \quad \text{for solidarity}\end{array}\right.$

THE ETHICS OF NATIONALISM

Speaking and writing in the early thirties, Tillich still entertained the possibility that Germans who were then opting for fascism as an organized cultural protest against bourgeois Enlightenment and its reifying impact might be persuaded to love justice and become socialists. This could happen, Tillich believed, if these people recognized that socialism, fully converted to the socialist principle, respects the particularity of cultural roots and draws upon the powers of land, people, and nation. The persons who truly love their land, its people and its culture, Tillich held, have a great desire that their country embody social justice. When later, in the mid-thirties, Tillich, then living in New York, was accused by Emanuel Hirsch, a well-known Protestant theologian turned Nazi, of having betrayed his country, Tillich replied that he was more faithful to Germany than his accuser: the person who loves his country best desires it to be just.[10]

Some readers may feel that Tillich's reflections on socialism and its need to be rooted in a myth of origin are no longer relevant in today's world. Socialism is a thing of the past. At the same time, the globalization of the capitalist economy is producing such disturbing results – widening the gap between rich and poor countries and between rich and poor in each country – that the utopia of an economic system based on cooperation instead of competition is not likely to disappear. This at least is the position developed in a recent book by the Canadian Protestant theologian Harold Wells.[11]

Why I regard Tillich's reflections as having great relevance for today's world is that they enable us to engage in intelligent dialogue with the contemporary movements inspired and guided by a myth of origin, be it religious, ethnic, regionalist, or nationalist. Liberals are unable to engage in such a dialogue: both political liberals, emphasizing universal values, and economic liberals, stressing material self-interest, regard people's attachment to historical roots as an obstacle to human progress. They want to rob people of their historical memories. They are not convinced – as were Buber, Gandhi, and Tillich – that people's creativity, their spiritual passions, and their access to the forces of life are derived from a myth of origin, that is to say, from their participation in a living tradition.

Tillich has demonstrated that a political project guided solely by a myth of origin has dangerous historical consequences, producing internal division and external aggression. To be ethical, or – more precisely – to serve human well-being at home and abroad, such a political project must be controlled by a myth of demand, an unconditional ethical ideal, or – in contemporary terms – a commitment to social justice and human rights. In Martin Buber's nationalism, the myth of unconditional demand was Prophetic Judaism; in Gandhi's nationalism it was non-violent Hinduism. For the Catholic bishops of Quebec, we recall from chapter 1, a nationalist movement was ethically acceptable only if its goal corresponded to the fourfold ethical proviso: creating a more just society, respecting the rights of minorities, cooperating with neighbouring countries, and refusing to make the nation the highest value.

5

Jacques Grand'Maison's Ethic
of Nationalism

Jacques Grand'Maison is a priest, theologian, political scien-
tist, and prolific author who is famous in Quebec, the largely
French-speaking Canadian province, but not well known in
the rest of the world. Since his numerous books deal with the
social, political, and religious issues arising in the changing
circumstances of Quebec society, they are of great local interest
and, for the same reason, have not attracted the attention of
readers in other countries. That none of his work has been
translated into English also reveals the cultural divide between
Quebec and English-speaking Canada. Jacques Grand'Maison
is learned, thoughtful, and practical. His special focus has
always been the lot of the little people, at the bottom and in
the margin, who have no one to take their side and speak for
them. Of particular interest to us in this chapter is his two-
volume work, *Nationalisme et religion*,[1] published in 1970, in
which he offers a historical interpretation of nationalism,
examines Christianity's relation to nationalist movements, and
explains why he, at the present moment, supports the nationalism of the Parti Québécois, Quebec's sovereignist political party.
In 1970, the Parti Québécois was a social democratic party. It
became the provincial government in 1976 and launched a

province-wide referendum on sovereignty-association in 1980, which it lost. A second referendum, in 1995, was also lost: support for sovereignty was only forty-nine per cent.

Grand'Maison's two-volume work does not deal with every aspect of Quebec nationalism, nor with all the issues addressed by the Parti Québécois, such as the equality of men and women, the right of the Native peoples to self-government, and the place of the English-speaking community in Quebec. Yet it deserves attention as it offers important reflections on nationalism and Christianity that have universal implications far beyond the Quebec context in which they were conceived and presented.

WHAT IS A NATION?

The first volume of Grand'Maison's *Nationalisme et religion* deals with nation, nationalism, and the creation of the nation-state. The author recognizes the polymorphous nature of these historical phenomena and that it is, therefore, very difficult to arrive at an agreement regarding the definition of the nation. What is a nation? For some people, a nation is a human community defined by a common origin, common historical experiences, common customs and styles, in most cases a common territory, and in many cases a common language or even a common religion. By contrast, for other people a nation is defined as a politically structured society that is conscious of its unity and sovereignly controls the territory it possesses. The first definition is historical, drawing upon memories and symbols of the past, while the second is political, based on the legislative power of the present.

In the province of Quebec, "nation" is used in the first sense, while in the rest of Canada, largely English-speaking, it is used in the second. Quebecers think of themselves as a nation, even those who are federalists and proud of being Canadian. In Quebec the provincial parliament is called "*l'assemblée nationale*," the provincial highways are "*les routes nationales*," and the provincial holiday is "*la fête nationale*." By contrast, English-speaking Canadians find it hard to understand how there can be more than one nation in a single state. Their "nation" is Canada. Today they are reluctant to recognize Quebec's claim to nationhood.

After the political upheavals in British North America, Lord Durham wrote in his famous 1839 Report for the British government, "I found two nations warring in the bosom of a single state." In 1867, at the time of Confederation, many Canadians recognized their new country as the union of two civilizations – or two races, as it was then called – defined by different languages, different ethnic origins, and different religions. George Brown, the voice of English Protestant Canada, rejoiced, "One hundred years have passed away since the conquest of Quebec, but here we sit, the children of victor and vanquished, all deliberating how a great people may be established on this continent."[2] George-Etienne Cartier, the leader of Quebec, also rejoiced: "The Catholic leaders of French Canada favour the new Confederation not only because we see in it so much security for all we hold dear, but because it does justice to our Protestant fellow-subjects as well."

Yet over the last decades Canadians have come to look upon their multicultural society simply as a country made up of ten equal provinces. Since Quebecers feel that this development robs them of their identity, they have put renewed emphasis on their nationhood.

Quebecers are not the only people who see themselves as a nation within a political state. Their situation is shared by the Scots and Welsh in Great Britain, the Catalans and Basques in Spain, and the Bretons and Corsicans in France. In Canada and the USA the Native peoples also claim to be nations and reach out for self-government. We may have to learn to speak of bi-national or even pluri-national countries.

Let me add to Grand'Maison's reflections that there also exists a Canadian nationalism, a current in Canadian political life that aims at protecting Canada's economy, its foreign policy, and its cultural institutions from being controlled by the United States of America.[3] Canadian nationalists want to prevent the cultural identity of their country from being dissolved by the growing political and commercial influence of their powerful southern neighbour. The Canadian Protestant theologian Douglas Hall has called this an instance of "nationalism at the edge of empire."[4] While a minority movement, Canadian nationalism has counted on the support of the New Democratic Party, Canada's equivalent of the British Labour Party, and a more recent organization, the Council of Canadians.

Grand'Maison recognizes that there is no purely objective definition of what a nation is. Every definition has concrete political implications and hence represents a political option. He mentions, for instance, that a minority can come to see itself as a nation when it has antagonistic relations with the dominant group or the government controlling it and if, for this reason, it wants to create its own sovereign state. He observes by way of contrast that the French-speaking community in Switzerland does not see itself as a nation. One might add that the Swiss Constitution has made it possible for the French-speaking community of the Jura to separate itself from the German-speaking canton of Berne to which it had belonged and constitute a canton of its own.[5]

The question of what is a nation raises important political issues. We saw that for Martin Buber, writing in the first decades of the twentieth century, the Jews constituted a nation in the modern, political sense, while his Jewish opponents saw the Jews quite differently. For some they were a religious community, while for others they were a community of fate, created by common memories and bearing an ethical message addressed to the whole of humanity. For Gandhi, the collectivity of Indian peoples constituted a single nation in the political sense, an idea that was shattered by the partition of India that came about with independence. Are the Palestinians a nation or an Arab minority living in the land of Palestine? Grand'Maison recognizes that nations are not a given, determined by their ethnic origin; nations are cultural constructions made under the pressure of historical circumstances.

NATIONALISM AND THE NATION-STATE

The next question posed by Grand'Maison is what is nationalism? Here again, he tells us, political thinkers entertain different definitions. After the experience of European and especially German fascism, some scholars define nationalism in pejorative terms as an ideology and a sentiment that exalts the nation, its history, its qualities, and its ambitions, often to the detriment of other nations.[6] A nationalist movement thus defined persuades people to look upon their nation as the supreme value and harbour contempt for other nations and for the minorities living in their midst. Here the nation becomes a dangerous idol.

Grand'Maison insists that this does not exhaust the meaning of the polymorphous phenomenon of nationalism. At the beginning of its history, nationalism referred to the struggle against the feudal order, the claim of popular sovereignty, the creation of the state, and the invention of responsible citizenship. Grand'Maison suggests that the first manifestation of this political struggle, prior to the American and French Revolutions, was the establishment, however brief, of the Puritan Commonwealth under Oliver Cromwell in the seventeenth century. The Puritans wanted Englishmen to be responsible citizens, not subjects of a king. After the American and French Revolutions, political and military struggles created sovereign nation-states on the European continent, among them Germany and Italy, while other European nations remained subjugated by empire, such as Ireland and Poland, yearning to achieve independent statehood in the future. The principle of national self-determination, Grand'Maison continues, was later endorsed by the American President Woodrow Wilson, and upon his insistence was applied, after World War I, to the nations formerly integrated into the Russian and Austrian empires.

What have these nationalist movements produced, Grand'Maison asks himself. They have created the modern state, he replies, which only too often has exercised arbitrary power, suppressed minorities, fought against its neighbours, and colonized peoples on other continents. Nations have become empires. The modern nation-states, moreover, were all created around certain centres of power so that they were, from the beginning, internally divided between regions of dominance and regions of dependency and underprivilege. This was true of the United States, France, Germany, and Italy. Grand'Maison adds that to protect its unity and promote its ambition, the state now encouraged nationalism as a sentiment and ideology that would make the people see themselves as superior to others and endowed with a political mission in the world. That which was good becomes evil. When a nationalist struggle for political self-determination achieves its aim, it easily turns into a movement of collective self-elevation justifying conquest and colonization.

Grand'Maison introduces the term "neo-nationalism" to designate the more recent national struggles in two different historical contexts, the first against colonial domination and the second against unitary state domination. He describes the struggles of colonies in Asia and Africa to become independent states, and the cultural and political efforts of peoples such as the Catalans and Basques in Spain, the Bretons and Corsicans in France, the Scots and Welsh in Britain, and the Quebec people in Canada to protect their collective identity. The world has, on the whole, been sympathetic to this neo-nationalism. In a covenant document the United Nations has recognized the right of peoples to political sovereignty: "All peoples have the right of self-determination. By virtue of the right they freely determine their political status and freely pursue their economic, social and cultural development."[7] The same document demands that the new governments respect the human rights of their citizens and protect the national minorities in their societies.

At the same time Grand'Maison does not idealize the neo-nationalist movements. The newly created states in Asia and Africa have tended to be dominated by their elites, to suffer internal divisions, and to adopt hostile attitudes toward their neighbours; the nations affirming their collective identity in unitary states have been tempted by self-absorption, narrowness of spirit, and xenophobia. Studying the histories of nationalism and neo-nationalism, Grand'Maison concludes, tends to make us sceptical in regard to their consequences. "*Le bilan historique est plutôt négatif*,"[8] the historical assessment is on the negative side. Only under special conditions, at a particular moment in history, a *kairos*, he argues, is it rational and ethically acceptable to support a nationalist movement.

CHRISTIAN FAITH AND NATIONALISM

In the second volume of his work Grand'Maison offers theological reflections on the relation of Christianity to nationalism. His emphasis is on the universalist dimension of the biblical message: all human beings are God's children, they constitute a single family, and all of them, without exception, command love and respect.

The Hebrew Scriptures record the story of a chosen people, a particular human community loved by God, yet – as Grand'Maison is quick to point out – the sacred text also reveals that the election of Israel is intended to be of service to the salvation of humanity. This universalist dimension had been greatly emphasized by the classical Hebrew prophets who saw God as sovereign of the universe standing for justice and extending mercy to all. Grand'Maison offers a long commentary on the book of Jonah, which mocks the parochialism of the hesitant prophet and proclaims God's universal mercy and care reaching even to the pagan city of Niniveh. It is possible to speak of an unresolved conflict in the Hebrew Scriptures between particularism and universalism.

This conflict also exists in the life of Jesus. According to the synoptic gospels, Jesus preached the coming of God's universal reign, a reign of justice and love, and at the same time restricted his ministry to members of his own people: "I have come to save the lost sheep of the house of Israel" (Matthew 10:6). It was only later when Paul preached the Good News to the nations that the overriding emphasis was placed on the universalist dimension. According to the Church's ancient dogma, the triune God, Creator, Redeemer, and Vivifier, embraces the whole of humanity and the entire cosmos. The human family is one in creation, one in original sin, and one in the economy of salvation.

Yet the Church in its historical existence, Grand'Maison continues, eventually fell back into particularism: it came to identify itself with the Roman Empire, despised the barbarians living beyond its borders, and attributed universal validity to the classical culture of Athens and Rome. Thus the old conflict between particularism and universalism continued in Christian history. As we shall see, Grand'Maison is very critical of the narrow particularism that, for a long time, dominated French-Canadian Catholicism. Yet despite these historical deviations there can be no doubt that the primary emphasis of orthodox Christian teaching is on the essential unity of the human family, created and redeemed by God, a unity that is in no way compromised by the subsequent division of human beings into tribes, nations, cultures, and religions. Universal love is the inescapable implication of Christian faith.

Grand'Maison arrives at the conclusion that Christians must stand against any theories and structures that undermine the unity of humankind, be they theories of cultural or biological superiority or political and/or economic institutions that divide the world into haves and have-nots. Christians must reject all form of prejudice. Christian universalism "calls for the defense of the lowest, the excluded, the most despised and opposes the spirit of party and class."[9]

Since Christianity must reject all attempts to narrow love and concern to specified limits and exclude certain groups of people from justice and equity, Christian faith has an antecedent suspicion of all forms of nationalism. Just as the study of nationalism persuaded Grand'Maison that its historical record leads to a rather negative assessment, so has his study of the Church's teaching convinced him that Christian faith must be suspicious of nationalism.

Still, Grand'Maison continues, in and by itself nationalism is not wedded to inequality nor opposed to universal solidarity. To demonstrate this, he now turns to the anthropological argument which we encountered in the chapter on Martin Buber. Humankind is made up of human beings not simply as individuals but as members of diverse cultural communities. Individuals are constituted by their integration into a community: they become persons by participating in given social institutions, a common language, a set of values and customs, and a cultural memory relating them to the past. The human spirit is always incarnate in a socially defined space: even personal self-knowledge is socially mediated through the symbols, values, and aspirations of the community. Personal identity is socially constructed. Personal creativity draws upon resources generated by the historical experiences and cultural heritage of one's people. We have called this the Durkheimian argument.[10]

In this context, Grand'Maison mentions Charles Taylor, the internationally known Montreal philosopher, who explains in his writings why, in modern times, individuals define their identity through the nation to which they belong. Taylor also explains why nations eventually aspire to self-government.[11] The Montreal philosopher, I must add, is a strong Canadian federalist who believes that slight changes in the Canadian Constitution would allow the people of Quebec to thrive as a nation within Canada. In his writings, Taylor shows that in reaction to the individualism of Hobbes, Locke, and other rationalist Enlightenment philosophers, the thinkers and poets known as the Romantics recognized that even in modern times people do not define their identity simply in terms of their material self-interest, but that this identity always includes cultural aspirations, historical memories, and horizons of meaning. While in medieval times people defined themselves through their place in the hierarchical cosmic order mediated by their Catholicism, in modern times people want i) to be faithful to their concrete existence, their own experiences, and the history that produced them, and ii) to create a community shaped by these cultural aspirations and capable of communicating them in the same language. The quest for nationhood is here experienced as part of an emancipatory process. In order to live authentically, in fidelity to their profound aspirations, people need institutions through which to express themselves and explore their heritage – schools, theatres, universities, parliaments, and many other services – and they demand that their language be the means of communication dealing with every aspect of their lives. They do not want their elites to go on speaking Latin or some other borrowed tongue. To create the appropriate institutions and ensure the free development of their genius, nations aspire to political self-government. Taylor regrets that English-speaking Canadians are reluctant to recognize Quebec as a people or nation within Canada. He has involved himself in public life to persuade Canadians to change their mind, accept the bi-national or even multinational character of Confederation, and rescue the country's political unity.

Charles Taylor here clarifies the Durkheimian argument by adding that only in modern times does the self-constitution of persons through their social matrix imply an orientation toward national self-government or state-formation.

Grand'Maison finds the Durkheimian argument confirmed by the Scriptures, since they present humanity as made up of different nations. While human sin has created enmity between nations, God has destined them to love justice, live in peace with one another, and to praise the Eternal One in a single voice. The God of the Bible loves nations and hates empires. We are told that empires, be they Egyptian, Babylonian, Assyrian, Persian, Macedonian, or Roman, are oppressors of nations and agents of violence and, because of their crimes, are doomed by God to destruction. God's judgment on empires is a theme running through the entire Scriptures, from the denunciation of Pharaoh who enslaved the people of Israel to the prediction of the downfall of Rome, heir of Babylon, in the book of the Apocalypse.

The antagonism between empire and nation has continued throughout history. It is my impression that a certain contemporary discourse that uncritically discredits all forms of nationalism reflects a largely unconscious identification with empire and with the peace imposed by empire in which nations survive as colonies or disappear altogether. It deserves attention that the small nations in Eastern Europe, Africa, and Asia that have recently embarked upon aggressive, vindictive, and irrational forms of nationalism have all been previously colonized by powerful empires, sometimes over periods of centuries. To humiliate a people is a dangerous political policy: it violates a human right and hence creates resentment and often, in the long run, irrational anger.

QUEBEC NATIONALISM PRIOR TO THE QUIET REVOLUTION

Major sections of Grand'Maison's two volumes are devoted to nationalism and religion in Quebec. While he is severe in his judgment of nationalism and the role of Catholicism in the old Quebec prior to the Quiet Revolution, he argues at length that in the situation of the sixties, a *kairos* in Quebec history, the nationalism of the Parti Québécois is a rational and ethical policy that deserves support.

Looking at the history of French Canada, Grand'Maison first examines French-Canadian nationalism after the Confederation of 1867 when French-Canadians – "*les canadiens*" in their own language – saw themselves as a nation, whose cradle and heartland was the province of Quebec, but whose members were spread over the whole of Canada. French-Canadian nationalism, at that time proud of Confederation, defended and promoted the national identity of all French-Canadians in the Canadian state, whether they were residents of Quebec or the other Canadian provinces. The political mission of this older nationalism was to sustain the French-Canadian presence in the whole of Canada and support the various institutions that served the French-Canadian communities, especially in Quebec.

Yet when the French school system in the provinces other than Quebec was gradually dismantled and the assimilation of French-Canadians into the English-speaking population kept on increasing, some French-Canadian leaders came to feel that the national culture of French-Canadians would survive only in Quebec, where they constituted the large majority and controlled the legislative assembly. In the twenties and thirties there emerged among certain leaders, including several priests, an ardent Quebec nationalism that favoured stronger self-government or even, for some, an independent state.

Grand'Maison offers a harsh critique of this movement. This nationalism, he explains, was guided by a conservative Catholic social philosophy that favoured a collectivist society committed to spiritual values and rejected modernity with its business orientation, its individualism and materialism, and its civil liberties and egalitarian ideals. This social philosophy reflected the hostile attitude adopted by the Catholic Church in the nineteenth century towards the arrival of modernity: the Church opposed the idea of popular sovereignty, the demand for democratic structures, the spread of industrialization, the expansion of urban life, the mobilization of the working class, and the respect for civil liberties, including the freedom of religion. The Church at that time categorically rejected socialism as well as liberalism. In the early part of the twentieth century, this highly conservative stance continued to be supported by reactionary Catholic groups in France and some other European countries; it found a North American expression in Quebec's Catholic nationalism.

Yet this movement represented a minority in Quebec: the bishops did not support it. Grand'Maison explains this by offering a critical analysis of the Church's role in the history of Quebec. Since the Church provided Quebec's social organizations, the institutions responsible for education, health care, social welfare, and cultural advancement, the Catholic clergy, omnipresent in the towns and villages, acquired an extraordinary cultural power. The Church became the backbone of this small, isolated nation on the North American continent. It defined its identity and assured its survival. Grand'Maison argues that the Church resisted all social change that threatened to reduce its power. The Church opposed the modernization of social life, assimilation into Canadian society, and the cultural influence of Protestants, Jews, and proponents of secularism. At the same time – Grand'Maison stresses this point – the Church supported Confederation and the British monarchy. Why? Because these institutions stood for legitimate rule blessed by God; they also protected the status quo and the Church's social power.

Still, the Church's conservative cultural vision prepared the ground for the Catholic nationalism of the twenties and thirties. Best known among these nationalists was Lionel Groulx, priest, historian, and social philosopher. He believed that Catholicism, its values and its structure, should become the basis of Quebec's national life. Grand'Maison offers this quotation: "Catholicism rules our entire life, it will always be the most active force among those that shape our society … Catholicism is the flying buttress of our race, its armour, its indefectible soul. We shall be Catholics or nothing at all."[12]

Since Lionel Groux called French-Canadians a race and authored a book called *L'appel de la race*, some commentators think of him as a racist in the contemporary sense of that term, i.e. committed to a theory dividing humanity into ethno-biological or ethno-cultural streams of unequal value and dignity. Is this a correct interpretation? We already remarked that Martin Buber used the word "blood" and Mahatma Gandhi the word "race" in a manner that has become offensive to our ears. In the past, these words had their own meaning. At the Canadian Confederation of 1867 many politicians spoke grandly of the reconciliation of the two races, British and French, a usage that continued into the twentieth century. Grand'Maison quotes a hostile remark of George Drew, the premier of the province of Ontario, uttered as late as 1936: "It is not improper to recall to the French that they are a conquered race and that their laws are laws only thanks to the tolerance of the English, who must, in all respect for the minority, be considered the dominant race."[13] Race here simply means people or nation defined by a common history.

Groulx appealed to many young people. He brought them a rich message, not all of which was reactionary. Young people were often ashamed of belonging to what North Americans regarded as a backward people. The eloquent priest persuaded them to be proud of their French and Catholic tradition that was spiritually superior to Protestant and secular North American culture. He also developed the anti-capitalist critique of Catholic social teaching, acknowledged the exploitation of working people, recommended a corporatist economy, and supported industrial development owned by French-Canadians. In the Depression this message appealed to many.

At the same time Groulx was strongly opposed to socialism, which he associated, following papal teaching, with secularism and godlessness. He favoured instead the corporatism recommended by Pope Pius XI, which envisaged the organization of the economy in corporations. These corporations, each made up of workers, managers, and owners belonging to the same branch or trade, were to constitute an economic council that would plan the national economy.[14] In Quebec the idea of corporatism was supported by many Catholic intellectuals and some politicians; business people and most politicians, however, were content with the capitalist system. Groulx was unhappy with economic liberalism and had a low opinion of democracy, which he regarded as government by the wealthy on their own behalf. He himself did not vote (except once toward the end of his life). He lamented that most French-Canadian politicians and business people, despite their Catholic faith and cultural difference, trusted economic liberalism and democratic rule. Since they were reconciled to the ways of North American society, he called them traitors. Traitors, for Groulx, were all French-Canadians who admired and imitated Anglo Protestant or secular styles of behaviour. He was also hostile to Jews whom he regarded as bearers of modernity and agents of pluralism.

According to Grand'Maison, Lionel Groulx preached a messianic nationalism. What does this mean? A political stance deserves to be called messianic, Grand'Maison explains, if it is guided by an unreachable utopia and lacks a rational political strategy. Groulx wanted Quebec to become a society in which the truth and values of Catholicism were to be fully incarnate. But how was this to come about? He had little sympathy for universal suffrage: as the Catholic Church was hierarchical, so should the nation be. God, Groulx believed, guides society through its leaders. Since democracy cannot help Quebec, Groulx hoped for the arrival of a charismatic leader close to God who would lift the people out of their present apathy, inspire them with his spiritual vision, and create for them an autonomous Catholic Quebec. This messianic nationalism made Groulx look with sympathy to fascist developments in Italy, Spain, and Portugal. Grand'Maison quotes the following text:

And you, young people, … act so that through your work and your prayer there may arrive for this sinking people the indispensable condition for its recovery; act so that there may arrive for us what has arrived in Portugal, Spain, Ireland, Poland, Italy, and even Turkey: a leader to train us and enkindle in us enthusiasm and political will.[15]

Yet this authoritarian nationalism found little resonance among ordinary people. It was not rooted in local communities nor connected to a political party. Action Libérale Nationale, a nationalist political party that had a brief existence in the thirties, rejected clerical influence, trusted the democratic process, dropped the idea of corporatism, and advocated instead a left-wing economic program.[16] In the absence of a strategy, Groulx's nationalism hoped for a miracle. The provincial government, whatever its rhetoric, liberal or conservative, encouraged liberal capitalism and sought to attract foreign investment by advertising the cheap and subservient labour force in Quebec. Maurice Duplessis, the authoritarian and reactionary premier of Quebec, did not have Lionel Groulx's approval since the premier, a ruthless pragmatist, was not a spiritual man.

In this context, Grand'Maison reflects on the political messianism often found among powerless people and humiliated minorities convinced that they have no chance to enter upon the scene of history by democratic means – means favoured by the successful countries that established their power by force a long time ago. Writing in 1970, Grand'Maison suggests that a similar messianism, even if totally secular, pervaded the revolutionary groups at that time which believed, quite irrationally, that Quebec could become a Marxist-style socialist society. For Grand'Maison, these groups are the atheist heirs of the totalitarian ideology of Catholic nationalism.[17] Groulx's nationalism of the thirties and the revolutionary socialism of the sixties, Grand'Maison argued, had no base among the people and hence little political influence. They represented the fervent imagination of a weak and humiliated people that had not yet achieved political maturity.

In the thirties, this Catholic nationalism was not the only vital movement in the Church in Quebec. Grand'Maison records that the orientation of Lionel Groulx was opposed by many Catholics who, influenced by theological currents coming from France, advocated dialogue with the modern world, supported freedom of thought and political pluralism, and saw themselves as participants in an international Catholic movement, reformist in orientation, promoting social justice in capitalist society. Lionel Groulx's counterpart was Georges-Henri Lévesque, the Dominican priest who founded a social studies institute at Laval University in Quebec City, and whose emphasis on democracy and participation was supported by wide circles in the Catholic Action movement. It was this current, swelling in the forties and fifties, that prepared the ground for the Quiet Revolution of 1960.

THE NATIONALISM OF
THE PARTI QUÉBÉCOIS

The cultural revolution beginning in 1960 revealed a profound transformation of Quebec society.[18] It manifested the people's political will to become responsible for their society, trust the democratic process, overcome the remnants of colonial subordination, and choose a government that would promote its economic and cultural advancement. The Quiet Revolution aimed at the modernization of Quebec: reforming the educational system, cultivating science and technology, and welcoming ideological and ethnic pluralism. At the same time, the Quiet Revolution wanted to save Quebec's heritage of solidarity and cooperation, resist North American individualism, and foster instead a social democratic ethos. Since the Vatican Council, taking place at that time, encouraged Catholic participation in reformist political movements, many engaged Catholics, including priests, brothers, and sisters, became actively involved in Quebec's cultural transformation. At the same time, reacting against the strict cultural control exercised by the Catholic Church in the past, an ever-growing number of Catholics turned to new freedom and adopted a secular outlook on life. Within the decade an unexpected, rapid secularization made practising Catholics a minority in Quebec.[19]

The Quiet Revolution, Grand'Maison argues, writing in 1970, has created the historical context in which nationalism, or more precisely the nationalist project of the Parti Québécois, has become a rational option. Several factors have converged to create the special conditions under which nationalism is an ethically acceptable policy. What are these factors? For Grand'Maison, they are first of all the commitment to democracy and the total absence of messianic expectations. Quebecers, he argues, have reached political maturity. The new nationalism, he repeats again and again, is not Catholic nor obsessed with the past. Nor is it defined by ethnicity. While Quebecers continue to see themselves as a nation rooted in history, they have become an open people welcoming others, of whatever religion or ethnic origin, as co-citizens living and working in the same society. Quebec's identity is becoming increasingly defined by common citizenship.

The reason why Quebec should now become a sovereign nation, Grand'Maison continues, is not because of national pride, sentimental attachment to the past, or a sense of spiritual or cultural superiority, but rather because this is the only rational manner in which to secure and protect its collective identity under the conditions of modernity. A sovereign state is needed to lift Quebec out of its dependent and disadvantaged position within the Canadian Confederation, an inheritance from the colonial past. The Quebec state must create a social democratic society in which French, the language of the majority, becomes the official tongue. The state must foster modernization and economic expansion, promote French-Canadian ownership and entrepreneurship, and use its legislative power to support the labour movement in its struggle for social and economic justice.

Could these changes not be introduced by Quebec's present provincial government? Grand'Maison replies that within the Canadian Confederation, Quebec's provincial government lacks the powers it needs to assume responsibility for several spheres of public life, such as employment, communication, economic development, and immigration, nor can it assign the French language its proper status. As an observer, I should report here that however unrealistic this may appear from Grand'Maison's perspective, there are many Quebec nationalists who do not aim at national sovereignty but instead favour a renewed federalism that will allow Quebec to protect its identity and develop its distinctive character.

Grand'Maison believes that the nationalist project of the Parti Québécois promised to be of advantage for Quebec and for English-speaking Canada. He envisages close economic cooperation between the two countries; he believes that getting rid of overlapping jurisdictions of the federal and provincial governments would be financially beneficial to both countries; and he argues that separation would enable Quebec as well as English-speaking Canada to develop a more confident and more vital collective identity, capable of resisting the cultural impact of the United States.

According to Grand'Maison, Quebecers had reached a turning point of their history, presenting them with three different options: i) integration into Canada as one of ten equal provinces, as proposed by Pierre Elliot Trudeau, then prime minister of Canada, ii) surrender to the individualistic techno-culture powerfully propagated in Canada through American media, American goods, and American advertising, and iii) sovereign national existence with economic association with Canada. Since the first option abandons the bi-national character of Canada, it would lead to gradual assimilation of Quebec into English-speaking Canada. The second option would lead in its own way to assimilation. Only the third option promises a future for Quebec society.

For Grand'Maison the seventies were a special moment, a *kairos*, in Quebec history when the nationalist option for sovereignty was the ethical choice demanded by reason. He rejoiced when in 1976 the Parti Québécois was elected to form the provincial government. In 1980 Grand'Maison strongly supported the referendum on sovereignty-association and criticized the Catholic bishops for refusing to take sides on this issue. We saw in chapter 1 that prior to this referendum, the Catholic bishops of Quebec affirmed the peoplehood of Quebecers and hence their right to self-determination, formulated a fourfold ethical proviso for nationalism in any form, but refused on principle to tell people how to vote.

Yet a special moment does not last forever. When, in its second mandate beginning in 1982, the Parti Québécois toned down its social democratic orientation and refrained from supporting the concerns of organized labour and the popular sector of society, Grand'Maison became an outspoken critic of the government. What had happened? Because the government had become the important agent promoting education, research, economic development, and cultural identity, it had created a new class of salaried employees, civil servants among them, who were now more concerned with their own advancement and security than with the tasks for which they had been appointed. In his writings, Grand'Maison calls them "*les promus de la révolution tranquille,*" those who profited from the Quiet Revolution, and he accuses this class of remaining indifferent to the majority of Quebecers, unorganized workers and low-income people in general.[20] Since the middle classes and organized labour were able to look out for themselves, Grand'Maison drew attention to the neglected sector of society as "*les tiers,*" the third ones – an allusion to the third world – and advocated community development and self-help initiatives in their neighbourhoods. Catholic parishes, he argued, should be in solidarity with *les tiers* and involve themselves in projects to rebuild community and foster a social economy.

This shift of perspective reduced Grand'Maison's trust in government and in solutions that are primarily political. Of greater importance for him were now social movements, the mobilization of communities, the involvement of citizens in cooperative action on every level of society. I do not know what relationship Grand'Maison had to the Parti Québécois in the eighties and nineties nor how he voted in the referendum of 1995. Did he think that the *kairos* in Quebec's history was still on, or did he believe that the special moment for choosing sovereignty had passed?

Since we are interested in Grand'Maison's reflections on nationalism, ethics, and Christian faith, let me return to his advocacy of Parti Québécois nationalism in his two-volume work of 1970. While he insisted that this political project was not Catholic but secular, sober, and rational, he believed that Catholics, summoned by the Vatican Council to assume reformist political responsibility, should join the nationalist movement. Christian faith, he had argued, inspires an antecedent suspicion in regard to nationalism since in so many cases it has sinned against the universalism proclaimed in the New Testament. Christians may in good conscience support nationalism only under very special conditions, conditions which he thought were fulfilled in the nationalist project of the Parti Québécois.

Jacques Grand'Maison decided to reprint in his two-volume work a theological statement on nationalism made by a group of Catholic theologians and published in *Le Devoir,* the distinguished Montreal newspaper, on 22 November 1969. The statement summarizes Grand'Maison's own reflections. The first part of the statement is, in my opinion, somewhat unclear because it hints at theological ideas without explaining their meaning. Still, the statement as a whole is an extraordinary public document on faith, ethics, and nationalism. It welcomes the nationalism of the Parti Québécois, it offers an analysis of how nationalism can become an evil force, and it tells Christians what influence they should exert within the nationalist movement. At the same time, the statement has universal implications. To my knowledge it has never been published in English.

The nation is the framework in which the human and Christian vocation normally finds its development. Since the reconciliation of humanity in God is a dimension of Christian hope, Christians realize more than others that nationalist movements belong to history and will disappear, after having prepared, if they were conducted with sanity, the great human unity destined for the end. That is why Christians set boundaries to their nationalism and reject any form of racism. Racism embodies the arrogant claim of a nation to a superior humanity, a claim the nation uses to defend social privilege and regard other people as instruments serving its own material advantage. At the same time, Christians do not expect the eschaton [the ultimate manifestation of God's reign] to be realized within their history. They recognize that the vocation of humanity is realized in concrete situations of cultural, linguistic, geographical and other diversities, and yet that these fecund diversities must not shut down the openness to the total human reality. Christians believe that they are called to be "the soul of the world," an expression used by the ancient church fathers who did not thereby declare themselves as citizens of the world. Christians need their homeland. It is precisely in being deeply rooted in where they are that their conscience matures, making them open to people everywhere. Their nationalism is therefore first respect for the collectivity to which they belong and which provides them with the vital milieu in which they develop as human beings. In the light of these reflections we as theologians feel at ease with the nationalist idea: at the same time we will not allow this idea to become an absolute, judging all things and not judged by anything. The nation is for us a servant of God and a servant of humanity. We will not allow that this idea replaces surreptitiously national pride with national arrogance which would make it into a kind of racism.

We want to gather the result of our reflections in a kind of decalogue. Nationalism and all the activities it entails are judged as human and Christian only if one can reply positively to the following ten questions:

1) Does this nationalism open the door to a cultural and human renewal following upon an antecedent stagnation, and does it have a realistic chance of success?

2) Has this nationalism developed as a reaction to an oppression or alienation that has over a considerable period of time harmed a fundamental human right?

3) Does it favour human equality and redistribution of wealth?

4) Does it favour healthy economic development and a stable form of human life?

5) Does it help the people involved in it to discover their true identity and freedom?

6) Will it attempt to open the nation to better relations with other cultures and with the whole of humanity?

7) Does it respect the rights of minorities, even while asking them to participate in the whole?

8) Does it recognize the legitimate autonomy of groups within the national community, respecting the rules of democracy and representation?

9) Will it attempt to integrate immigrants, offering them the same chances of equality and development?

10) Will it support the creation of an authentic culture as the context in which the human vocation can find its development?[21]

6

Conclusions, Proposals, and Unresolved Questions

In this concluding chapter I shall engage with the four thinkers whose ethics of nationalism we have examined in the preceding chapters. While Buber, Gandhi, and Grand'Maison were committed nationalists, Tillich was not: he appreciated nationalism, believed that liberals and socialist were wrong in discrediting it, and formulated an ethical imperative to which any myth of origin must be subordinated. In my opinion, our four authors would have agreed with the fourfold ethical proviso for nationalism proposed by the Catholic bishops of Quebec:[1] a nationalist movement is ethically acceptable only if it advocates a more just society, respects the minorities, intends to cooperate with its neighbours, and refuses to regard the nation as the highest good.

THE SINISTER SIDE OF NATIONALISM

The first question I wish to pose is whether these four thinkers have adequately explored the dark side of nationalism and duly warned the world of its evil consequences. Buber, we noted, did not develop this dark side in his speeches before World War I. He then referred with approval to nationalist movements in Europe that were critical of secular modernity and called for a return to spiritual values and national heritage. In this context, he lauded Charles Péguy. Yet Buber did not say a word about the conservative Catholic nationalism, a powerful political force in France, which was opposed to democracy and pluralism, and antisemitic into the bargain. Similar movements existed in other European countries. After the war, in 1921, Buber did recognize that once its primary goal is achieved, nationalism easily produces an ideology of aggression and hostility. Yet he used his exploration of the dark side of nationalism mainly as a critique of trends in the Zionist movement and not as a warning against dangerous trends in nationalist movements in Europe. He did not reflect in this context on the spread of antisemitism. The reason for this may well be that Buber attributed the alienation of the Jews in European society to the impact of secular modernity and the neglect of their own spiritual tradition. He wanted the Jewish people to define their identity by a return to their own prophetic inheritance, not by a response to the hostility to which they were exposed. That is, I think, why Buber's critique of nationalism was mainly directed to his own Zionist movement.

Because Buber demanded, from the very beginning, respect for the local Palestinian community, he became, despite his brilliance and his Zionist passion, a marginal figure in the Zionist movement. Much later, after the foundation of the State of Israel, he became a vocal critic of Israeli nationalism. A close collaborator of his, Ernst Simon, a friend from the twenties in Germany who himself became an important critical thinker in Israel, is credited with this quotation: "When we were young, we believed we could pick the raisins out of the poisonous cake of nationalism; now that we are old, we recognize that even the raisins were poisoned."[2] Buber and many of his followers took the risk of nationalism because they believed that this was God's will.

For Gandhi the dark side of nationalism was hatred and violence, a behaviour at odds with Hindu piety. Hatred and violence were un-Indian. We noted that in his *Hind Swaraj* Gandhi mentioned more than once that he felt no hostility for the English. He pitied them; he believed they had been robbed of their religious and ethical tradition by modern civilization. What he fought against was a system of domination, a set of institutions operating according to a logic of its own. Gandhi believed that his discovery of *satya/graha,* or truth-force, created a nationalist movement, different from all others, that nourished respect for the colonial oppressor and demanded from its adherents gentleness, self-discipline, and the spirit of sacrifice. Yet we also noted that Gandhi, while rejecting modern civilization, was not fully aware that setting up an independent nation-state, the aim of his nationalist movement, is a modernizing process that would inevitably bring to India structures of domination at odds with his own communitarian and anarchist ideas. We saw that, in arguing with the poet Tagore, Gandhi confessed that he took the risk of nationalism because he believed there was no other way to rescue the masses of India from their misery.

Writing his book while the Nazis were marching in the streets, Tillich was well aware of the dark side of nationalism. He argued in systematic fashion that any political movement steered exclusively by a myth of origin, national, ethnic, or religious, was dangerous: it would inevitably lead to external aggression and internal oppression. War and apartheid would be its fruit. Yet Tillich did not follow the majority of anti-fascist thinkers: he did not discredit nationalism as such. He honoured the myth of origin of any people. What he demanded was the strict subordination of nationalism to the norms of social justice, equality, and international peace. Tillich looked upon modernity as bearing within itself a myth of demand, derived from biblical sources, generating a restless, never-to-be-satisfied yearning for humanity's redemption from injustice.

Writing after World War II and the horror of Nazism, Grand'Maison adopted a cautious tone in regard to nationalism. Its dark side was ever before him. The historical balance sheet of nationalism was on the negative side, he wrote. Christians in particular, following the universalist vision of their faith, should have an antecedent suspicion in regard to nationalism. Still, there were special moments and special situations when it was both rational and ethical for a people to turn to nationalism and reach out for political sovereignty. For social, political, and cultural reasons, Grand'Maison argued at length, the right time, the *kairos*, for straining after Quebec sovereignty had arrived. Since he recognized the risks this involved, he not only spelled out the ethical norms to which nationalism must be subject but also laid bare the mental mechanisms by which nationalism threatens to turn into arrogance, xenophobia, and racism. Grand'Maison's ethical proposal fits perfectly into Tillich's theoretical perspective.

NATIONALISM NOT AT ODDS
WITH UNIVERSALISM

The second issue I wish to discuss is the idea, shared by our four authors, that nationalism is not at odds with universalism or universal solidarity. Buber strongly emphasized this idea. He argued at length that human beings are integrated into humanity not as single individuals but as members of different peoples or cultural communities. I have called this the Durkheimian argument. Nationalism recognizes the pluri-national condition of humanity and hence, in and by itself, is international in outlook. Buber put this principle into practice when he stood up, from the very beginning, for the rights of the Palestinians and remained faithful to them for the rest of his life.

Gandhi, in his dispute with Tagore, also stressed the bonds of solidarity that united the Indian nationalist movement with peoples in other parts of the world struggling against the domination of modern empire. Gandhi even believed that his version of Indian nationalism contained a message of universal significance. His advocacy of a subsistence economy in the villages and a spiritual life of self-discipline may need to become the cultural formula for the rest of the world, seeing that the quest for material progress invented by the West cannot be universalized. Restless Western development is a way of death. For Gandhi nationalism and universal solidarity went hand in hand.

Grand'Maison, we noted, used the Durkheimian argument to show that nationalism and internationalism can and should go together. In fact, the Durkheimian argument suggests that undifferentiated universalism is an ideology of domination. To praise cosmopolitanism or universal humanism and assert that we are all citizens of the world is a political message that intends to cut people loose from their cultural roots and assimilate them to a certain Western-style self-understanding. Our four authors would agree that every undifferentiated universalism is an arrogant particularism intent on making itself the norm for the whole of humanity. Grand'Maison recalled the hidden ideology of the classical humanism of Greece and Rome that presented itself as the universal measure and entertained contempt for the barbarians beyond the frontier. Grand'Maison added that in the early centuries the Christian Church became profoundly influenced by this ideology.

Following the same line of thought, Tillich showed that economic liberalism, political liberalism, and Marxism presented concepts of humanity that made attachment to cultural roots and national identity appear reactionary, an obstacle to human progress. Economic liberals defined humans by their struggle to improve the material conditions of their lives – yet if utility is the highest value, then old-fashioned people still attached to the traditions of their community lead economically irrational lives. Reason would eventually teach them to bracket their inherited loyalties.

Democratic liberals – I am here following Tillich's vocabulary – also despised people's attachment to tradition. Theirs was a universalism based on freedom, equality, and responsible citizenship: on universal values that liberated people from conformity to received values, feudal inequalities, and the passive acceptance of their cultural inheritance. Memories of the past were important to political liberals only when they served the creation of the nation-state, its unity and its glory. With his contempt for the past, Karl Marx still belonged to the early phase of the Enlightenment. He believed, at least according to some of his texts, that by their nature people were driven to promote the material advantage of their economic class and that this drive assured the victory of the many at the bottom over the few at the top, leading ultimately to a classless society. He regarded the attachment to religious, ethnic, or cultural roots as an ideology protecting the power of the ruling class: among working people, he believed, such an attachment is an obstacle to the class struggle and hence to human progress. We noted that in 1932 Tillich, then a supporter of working-class struggle, argued that Marx had misunderstood the workers: Marx did not realize that the motives for their struggle included attachment to their cultural home and the fear of its loss through the impact of industrial growth along capitalist lines. At that time, Tillich believed that socialism could succeed only if it learnt to appreciate the rootedness of people in their tradition.

Our four authors agree that the narrowness and arrogance so often associated with nationalism cannot be overcome by an emphasis on cosmopolitanism, globalization, world citizenship, or any form of undifferentiated universalism. Such forms of universalism are particularisms straining after universal power. Successful classes have always tended to regard their own self-understanding as the definition of human nature. Our four authors believed that the temptation of narrowness and arrogance present in nationalist movements must be overcome by the recognition of the pluri-national character of humanity. Using plain theological language, Buber wrote that God had created humanity as many nations.

NATIONS ARE HISTORICALLY CONSTRUCTED

At the same time – this is the third issue I wish to discuss – our four authors agree that nationhood is something constructed. The nation, they concur, is not something natural defined by biological inheritance. The Durkheimian argument, as we saw above, states that people enter into their humanity by participation in a particular community. Humans acquire consciousness through the language and other signs and gestures of the community in which they are raised. But such a community need not be a nation: it might be an extended family, a tribe, a group of people united by loyalty to the same prince, or some other integrated collectivity. Nations, like other communities, are historically constructed.

In this entire study, we have looked upon nationalism as a post-feudal, modern phenomenon and hence acknowledged the nation as a modern construction. We have noted many times that there is no perfect agreement on what a nation is and that every definition of it carries a certain concrete political meaning. Yet all the authors agree that nations are constituted by a set of objective and subjective factors, where the objective factors include a common heritage, usually a common territory, often a common language, a governing centre, and a network of economic institutions; the subjective factors include a vision of society, a set of symbols, and the political will to be a nation. Nations are "imagined communities," following Benedict Anderson's oft-cited terminology.[3] They are imagined insofar as they create a sense of comradeship among people who have never met, define boundaries that are not given by nature but by convention, and persuade people that they have the right to determine their future.

Buber, Gandhi, and Grand'Maison would not have objected to the term "imagined community." Buber believed that the Jews still had to create themselves as a nation. Through conversion to the highest moments of their tradition, Prophetic Judaism, the Jews had to acquire the will to become a nation. We noted that, at the beginning of the century, most Jews did not see themselves as a nation in the political sense. They thought of themselves as a religious community or a community created by a common history and defined by a common destiny. It was only after Nazi persecution and the Holocaust that Zionism became the political option of the majority of Jews.

Gandhi also recognized that the Indian nation is a constructed reality, grounded in a common heritage and yet still to be realized in history by a common will and common action. We saw that Gandhi refused to believe that the nation of India was constructed by the British imperial presence which had created unifying institutions in their vast colony and at the same time provoked common resistance against the colonizing power. Gandhi stressed the shared cultural heritage of Hindus and Muslims and demanded personal conversion to self-discipline, away from the Western ideal of self-expansion. *Swaraj* or self-government was personal before it could become political.

Jacques Grand'Maison also recognized that the nation of Quebec was a constructed reality. In fact, he compared it with a previous French-Canadian nationalism that sought to enhance and protect the collective identity of French-Canadians in the whole of Canada.

Our four authors would not have disagreed with Max Weber's thesis that even ethnicity is not biologically defined but constructed. Writing at the turn of the century when *"völkisch"* or ethnic movements sought political power in Germany and other European countries, Weber argued that ethnicity refers to groups of people that believe they are derived from the same blood line. Ethnicity is constituted by the belief, not the fact, of biological inheritance.[4]

At the same time, our authors did not think that because nations were constructed, they were artificial creations over and against some sort of natural order. To recognize nations as constructed does not mean that they are either distorted realities or purely external frames of reference imposed upon their members. After all, languages are constructed and so are families. Languages, families, tribes and, in the modern period, nations are historically constituted by a combination of material and mental factors that allow individuals to enter upon their humanity. Our four authors would not be sympathetic to the ideas of Ernest Gellner and Eric Hobsbawm who, in their studies of nationalism, have emphasized the element of manipulation and fabrication in the construction of nations.[5]

Arguing against Gellner's and Hobsbawm's suspicions I would ask how else could a people under the impulse of modernity have acquired collective self-responsibility, except through the creation of an appropriate political structure, in most cases a sovereign state? This process undoubtedly included a certain element of force and propaganda. Punishment awaited Americans opposed to Independence and death and exile Frenchmen who stood in the way of the Revolution; pressures were put on Germans and Italians who resisted the creation of the nation-state. Among our authors, it was Grand'Maison who explored the ambiguous character of nationalism and the sovereign nation. Political states were created around centres of political and industrial power that produced regional inequalities and exploited classes in the new nations. Yet this did not invalidate the essential thrust of nationalism: the people who now experienced themselves as a nation were able to engage in political action to overcome inequality and exploitation and transform their nation into a more just society. Nationalism has moved Western society from feudalism to an international order. While this process was by no means unilinear, few people are ready to believe that the sovereign state based on law is a more distorted historical formation than the aristocratic or colonial regimes which it has replaced.

At present just about the whole world has become an international order – over sixty new states have been created since World War II. At the same time, something altogether new is taking place, the as yet largely unexplored phenomenon of globalization. Will it generate nationalist reactions of a new kind?

DOES CONTEMPORARY GLOBALIZATION DISSOLVE NATIONAL COHESION?

Let us look at two arguments proposing that in today's world people no longer define themselves through participation in a national community.

The *first argument* insists that we are presently witnessing the spread of a utilitarian techno-culture on a global scale that allows people to choose their spiritual horizon, their values, and their lifestyle quite independently from the culture they have inherited. What shapes people's lives is no longer membership in a cohesive national community but rather participation in a global culture created by technology, competition, and a cornucopia of consumer goods. The Weberian critique of modernity, now applied to the globalized society, is here seen as invalidating the Durkheimian argument. National cohesion disappears. We witness the weakening of many traditional institutions, family, church, and nation, making room for alternative forms of community. Some authors call this the postmodern condition.

There are two differing interpretations of this global or incipiently global phenomenon. One of them is totally negative. The universal mono-culture, it is being argued, sustained by the centres of economic and technological power, and in particular by the one remaining superpower, offers the freedom to choose an independent, creative lifestyle only to certain elites that can afford independence from their environment, people who have a good income, can travel, have leisure or interesting work and can choose to live where they like. Yet for the great majority, the impact of the global mono-culture is an initiation into emptiness and superficiality. We recall that Martin Buber denounced the alienating force of the spreading techno-culture and praised as a spiritual response to this the return to roots and to nationalism in particular. Gandhi, we remember, was even more vehement in his reaction. He called the mono-culture mediated by the British empire "satanic" because, by appealing to people's love of gain and pleasure, it had already destroyed the ethical cultures of Europe shaped by the Christian tradition, and was presently undermining the ancient ethical cultures derived from the religions of India. We saw that, according to the Weberian critique of modernity, forced conformity to instrumental rationality pushed contemporary society into "an iron cage." Today, Jürgen Habermas accuses the rationalization and bureaucratization of public and private institutions of "colonizing the life world," i.e. subjecting people to a rationality at odds with the rhythm and the breath of life.

Yet there exists also a more positive interpretation of contemporary globalization. Transnational capitalism and the omnipresence of techno-culture weaken many of the inherited institutions, including in particular the state, thus making room for the emergence of imaginative, small-scale alternatives to universal control. The postmodern French philosopher Jean-François Lyotard has argued that since the course of the world is now determined by technologized economic processes from which the majority of people, and even national governments, are excluded, political, society-transforming projects, liberal or socialist, have become outmoded.[6] What remains possible, the postmodern critics hold, is the creation of new and imaginative communities enabling their members to live culturally rich lives. This, it is argued, is the good news of postmodernity. The new Scottish nationalism, which I mentioned in chapter 1, sees itself as a postmodern phenomenon: a little nation, constrained in a unitary state, having the courage to create an alternative. There seems to be much evidence that despite the globalization of capitalist culture, people still want to define themselves through fidelity to their national identity and their cultural or religious inheritance – in Tillich's terminology, their myths of origin.

A *second argument* proposes that the Durkheimian theory, according to which humans enter upon their humanity through integration into a cultural community or nation, is no longer true. Population mobility has become global. In fact, Durkheim's anthropological theory has often been questioned by people who as immigrants or refugees have had to move from one country to another or whose parents belonged to different cultures and who, therefore, did not define themselves as members of a single community. Where does this anthropological theory say to them? Does it imply that they are in some way incomplete? Are they branches cut from a tree unable to bear fruit? Are they cut flowers destined to fade away? Since my own biography is situated across nations and communities, this question is of special interest to me.

In my opinion, the anthropological argument explains very well what people marked by this fate do to overcome their experience of homelessness. Some of them cling to their original inheritance, even at the cost of remaining strangers in their new location. Others make a great effort to root themselves in their new cultural tradition, its language, its literature, and its values. Others again seek a firmer identification with a transnational cultural matrix, for instance science, liberalism, or Marxism – or a world religion, preferably their own. All of them, in one way or another, testify that personal expansion and creativity takes place through rootedness in a great tradition.

DO LIBERALS WANT TO STEAL PEOPLE'S HISTORY?

In this section I wish to examine the distinction between ethnic and civic nationalism, the former being based on ethnic origin and the latter on common citizenship. This distinction is useful. Ethnic nationalism tends to be narrow, exclusive, and xenophobic, while civic or liberal nationalism embodies democratic ideals and welcomes the participation of all citizens. Grand'Maison, as we saw, contrasted Quebec's narrowly ethnic and Catholic nationalism of the twenties and thirties with its increasingly civic or liberal nationalism of the present, open to pluralism. In Michael Ignatieff's recent work on the emerging nationalist currents in the former Yugoslavia and Soviet Union, this distinction plays a major role: ethnic nationalism is bad while civic nationalism is, at least under certain circumstances, acceptable.[7]

Still, our four authors would not have accepted the neat opposition between ethnic and civic nationalism. This opposition suggests that civic nationalism is simply a political ideal based on common citizenship and hence must become indifferent to its historical origin. Yet, in fact, nations do remember the ethnic tradition that has shaped them in the past. The American Revolution reflected a culture with roots in a particular British Protestant tradition, Puritan and Methodist, known for its independence, its contestation, and its will to transform society. Because a nation is open to the participation of all citizens does not mean that it ceases to remember and celebrate its historical origin. The civic nationalism that has created liberal society continues to have ethnic memories. Gandhi, we remember, entertained an idea of the Indian nation so wide that even Englishmen willing to adopt the Indian ethos could become part of it; at the same time, he remained attached to the national traditions of India as sources of inspiration. Grand'Maison's nationalism, which welcomed as equal citizens people of whatever origin, was rooted nonetheless in the historical evolution of the French colony settled in the seventeenth century on the soil of the Amerindian peoples. The neat opposition between ethnic and civic nationalism is easily used as an ideological weapon by liberals and socialists to make people feel guilty over their attachment to their national tradition.

The heirs of Enlightenment rationalism, liberals and socialists, tend to see people's fidelity to their cultural and religious inheritance as reactionary, an obstacle to the aims of the republic. In chapter 1, I mentioned Charles Péguy, strong defender of the republican virtues, who became so unhappy with the republican policy to dismiss as irrational and therefore suppress the ordinary people's religious culture that he eventually became a nationalist, a defender of religion, even a man of faith, all the while remaining open to pluralism. Péguy recognized that the republican contempt for people's cultural and religious legacy drove many of them to stubborn resistance in the form of narrow, xenophobic, anti-republican nationalism. His observation articulates a principle that may well have universal application.

Since the government of India, following a spirit different from Gandhi's, opted for a civic nationalism devoid of historical roots and hence defined itself in purely secular terms, it did not honour the country's religious believers, that is the great majority of the people. Since the Hindu population experienced itself as strangers in their own country, many of them have come to adopt belligerent and intolerant positions, at odds with their own millennial tradition.

Paul Tillich analysed this phenomenon in systematic fashion. Political projects defined by a "myth of demand" – liberalism and socialism – tend to despise people's attachment to "myths of origin," be they ethnic, cultural, religious, or a mixture of these. But because the ordinary people remain attached to their human inheritance, their home, their land, and their culture, they frequently resist progressive political projects and turn to reactionary movements defined exclusively by a myth of origin. Tillich argued that many Germans living in small towns and villages and even active members of the working class were attracted by the Nazi rhetoric because liberals and socialists, thinking in universalist terms, had no respect for their particular communities. I already mentioned another anti-fascist author, Karl Polanyi, writing in the thirties, who denounced fascism as the distorted return of the repressed. The repressed here refers to the communitarian dimension of human life, disregarded by abstract liberalism (the person as citizen or the person as actor in the market) and ideological socialism (the person embedded in his or her economic class). In German fascism, Polanyi argued, the repressed dimension returned in a distorted form, demanding the annihilation of the individual in the collectivity.

What I conclude from our four authors is that it is misleading to make a neat opposition between ethnic and civic nationalism. Even a civic nation defined by common citizenship remains attached to and celebrates its historical evolution, including its ethnic or religious origin.

Ideological liberals want to rob people of their history. Let me illustrate this with examples from Canada. Quebec nationalism, as we saw above, is civic, democratic, and open to pluralism, yet remains grounded in a particular history which it remembers and celebrates. In the 1980s, the Quebec government defined the pluralistic nature of Quebec society by distinguishing between the host culture and the cultural communities of more recent origin and promoted dialogue and cooperation between them. This intercultural process was intended to transform both the host culture and the cultural communities, bringing them closer together without thereby losing their identity.[8] Quebec sees itself as a pluralistic society. Yet when Quebecers whose ancestors arrived from France over three centuries ago call themselves "*québécois de souche*," Quebecers of old stock, they are often criticized by English-speaking Quebecers of being narrow, ethnocentric, or even racist: these critics seem to believe that living in an open, pluralistic society means that Quebecers of old French origin, the large majority, should give up being attached to and celebrating their history. Yet what the old Quebecers wish is that new Quebecers join in celebrating the history of their common society. Even the reluctance of English-speaking Canadians to recognize Quebec as a nation or people is based, in part at least, on an ideological liberal position demanding that Quebec no longer define itself out of its three and a half century old history in North America. Liberal individualism and liberal universalism want to deprive people of their particular history. While there exists indeed an attachment to history that is closed and reactionary, there is also a fidelity to history that is open and creative.

In this study I am not dealing with the right to self-government of the First Nations. Reduced in number and culturally damaged by their oppressors, they are presently experiencing a rebirth and the reaffirmation of their national identities. Because they must rescue themselves from social forces that almost destroyed them, their nationalism is out-spokenly ethnic. Unless they protect their bloodline, they shall disappear. While this seems ethically legitimate to me at this time, I think that in the long run the Native peoples will want to examine more carefully how to define the boundaries of their communities. Ideological liberals have little sympathy for the struggle of the First Nations. There even exists a Canadian association that, in the name of liberal theory, denies the legitimate claims of the First Nations to land and self-government: the association argues that since Canada is a liberal democracy with equality before the law of all its citizens, Canada cannot recognize collective rights based on a common history: Amerindians will have to become Canadians like everyone else.

THE PERSPECTIVAL READING OF HISTORY

Our four authors also acknowledge that there is no perfectly objective manner of reading history. The reading of the past and present is always guided by certain paradigms or heuristic concepts that are inevitably charged with political meaning. Thus the American and the French Revolutions and the American Civil War continue to be interpreted by historians in different ways, giving rise to a debate that cannot be resolved by purely scientific means. The reading of history, however faithful to the objective norms of historical research, inevitably reflects both the scholar's social location and his or her political option. When Buber, Gandhi, and Grand'Maison present the history of their people, they fully realize that there exist alternative readings. Buber presented the assimilation of Jews into Western society as an entry into modern alienation, while other Jewish scholars, more open to the positive side of modernity, especially democracy and pluralism, reported the history of Jewish assimilation in different terms. Gandhi preferred historians who uncovered evidence in antiquity for the cultural unity implicit in India's linguistic, religious, and ethnic traditions. Grand'Maison realized that the historians on whom he relied were not the only scholarly interpreters of Canadian history.

Some historical events give rise to differing interpretations at the very moment they occur. One of these is the Canadian Confederation of 1867 which was seen by some as the union of two civilizations, British and French, and by others as the federation of four provinces. It is not surprising that the history taught in the province of Quebec differs from the history taught in the other Canadian provinces. An important ethical issue for nationalism, as I see it, is the question how it sees "the other."

Is it possible for nations with a history of competition or enmity to produce a history of their interrelation over decades and centuries acceptable to both sides? Today Protestant and Catholic historians have achieved a remarkable consensus in presenting the Protestant Reformation. In the long process of German-Polish reconciliation after World War II, a commission of German and Polish historians examined the history books used in the schools of both countries and tried to arrive at a historical account of German-Polish relations since the Middle Ages acceptable to the self-understanding of both Germans and Poles.[9] A school book research institute in Germany continues to examine cross-border school books and, with the help of cross-border scholars, propose improvements that are historically faithful and at the same time foster respect for their neighbour.[10]

What is the philosophical conviction behind research projects that want to respect the historical perspective of two national, ethnic, or religious communities at odds with one another? Such a project is impossible if the participants believe that an evolutionary thrust, defined by the survival of the fittest, constitutes the driving force of human history. Nor is it possible if the participants hold the view that human progress is served by a single tradition: a nation, a church, or a culture. Research of this kind, it seems to me, is inspired by a utopian vision of humanity marked by pluralism and cooperation and by the conviction that competing interests will not be solved by the victory of the strong over the weak, but by a common commitment to justice and eventual reconciliation. The documents of the United Nations reveal such a perspective. Yet that this is the truth about humanity cannot be scientifically demonstrated: it is a faith rather than the conclusion of an empirical investigation. Our four authors, all of them religious believers, are convinced that present in history is a reconciling Transcendent summoning people everywhere to justice, pluralism, and respect for the other.

It is an ethical imperative for any nationalism to make room in its reading of history for "the other." Buber wanted the Zionist movement from the beginning to recognize and respect the presence of the Palestinian population. Gandhi insisted that his fight was against British imperialism, not against the English people whose traditional roots he greatly respected. Grand'Maison argued, as we noted, that Quebec sovereignty would be advantageous for English Canada, making it easier for its people to define their culture, resist American influence, and affirm their own, original identity. If people fail to recognize "the other" in their own self-definition, the other soon becomes the opponent or even the enemy. This issue is an issue not touched at all in Émile Durkheim's understanding of society. He saw the nation as an autonomous society whose relation to other societies was accidental and not of the essence. Perhaps it is only the interdependence of all societies recently produced by the complex process of globalization that has created the social conditions in which relation to "the other" enters into a society's own self-understanding.

AN ECONOMY THAT SERVES THE NATION

Our four authors also had ethical positions regarding the economy. Buber regarded himself as a socialist. We saw that he advocated a socialism from "the bottom up," a cooperative, decentralized economic system protected by government. Buber's ideal was part of the Zionist project as he saw it, embodied in the kibbutzim founded in Palestine. Gandhi, we recall, was a radical opponent of industrial capitalism: he believed that the great masses of India could survive and lead a dignified life only if all Indians practiced self-restraint and protected the subsistence economy of the Indian villages. When Tillich wrote the book we have studied, he regarded himself as a revisionist Marxist. Grand'Maison as a social democrat believed that a strong government supported by the people could restrain and guide capitalism to make it serve the well-being of society as a whole. For the four authors nationalism was ethically acceptable only if it stood for social justice and the fair distribution of wealth. In an interesting paragraph, Gandhi was critical of Garibaldi who, using force, united Italy and freed certain parts of it from Austrian rule but was unconcerned about justice and freedom. "If you believe," Gandhi writes, "that because Italians rule Italy the Italian nation is happy, you are groping in darkness."[11] By contrast, Gandhi had sympathy for Manzini's political ideals that included economic justice.

In many instances, nationalism has economic implications. First, a nationalist movement is often associated with an economic project believed to serve the nation as a whole. In its struggle against the feudal order, nationalism usually supported capitalist industrial development, trusting that it would produce the wealth needed to modernize the nation. When a new kind of nationalism reacted against modern individualism and the culture produced by capitalism, it often proposed alternative models of economic development. Buber was committed to utopian socialism. Prior to World War I, many nationalists belonging to nations integrated into the Austrian and Russian empires struggled for national liberation and a socialist economy. In France, some nationalists promoted syndicalism. After the war, Italian-style fascism proposed a corporatist organization of the industries under the control of the state. The corporatism recommended by Pope Pius XI which, as we saw above, was supported by Catholic nationalism in Quebec, differed from fascist corporatism inasmuch as Catholic teaching envisaged the national economic council representing corporations as independent of the state, not, as the fascists wanted it, directed by the state. Welfare capitalism based on the theory of John Maynard Keynes recognized government intervention, respect for working-class power, and a certain economic protectionism favouring the national economy. For this reason, welfare capitalism, especially if steered by a social democratic government, lent itself to nationalist aspirations. The Quebec nationalism supported by Grand'Maison stood in this tradition. Nationalism by its very nature, it would seem, is opposed to the globalization of free trade, the rule of the self-regulating market system, and the subsequent inability or unwillingness of governments to protect the economic well-being of their people.

Yet nationalism can be related to the economy in another way. Social solidarity and the will to succeed collectively associated with nationalist movements often prompt people to become inventive and work harder. In Spain the Catalans and the Basques have produced important industrial centres. Finland and other small European nations are economically successful because they do not take their survival for granted but struggle to preserve their autonomy. After World War II the Austrians, for obvious reasons, wanted to define their national identity totally independent of Germany and thus created an industrial development that was only minimally related to the German industries. This nationalist project released great energy and led to remarkable economic success. The literature of the Parti Québécois has expressed a similar hope.[12] It has been argued that large European countries like Britain and France have faltering economies because their widely spread industries can no longer be surveyed and guided, and because their workers do not feel that their labour contributes to their country's collective identity. By contrast, the argument goes on, many of the small European countries with their survey-able industries and their nationally committed workers enjoy a healthier economy. While mainline economists think that labour is always motivated by material self-interest, other economists recognize the complexity of human motivation. Karl Polanyi has argued at length that prior to the arrival of industrial capitalism, the motive making the ordinary people work was mainly integration into their community and the recognition and respect with which this was rewarded. Motivation was social, rather than economic.

NATIONALISM AND LANGUAGE

Nationalism is closely related to language. In the American republic English became the common language, and in the French republic it was the French spoken in the region of Paris, overshadowing other tongues used in France. Buber took for granted that the Jewish nation would become united in the single language of modern Hebrew. Making this new tongue the universal language of the State of Israel has been a major histor-ical achievement, even if it demanded a sacrifice from Eastern European Jews who cherished Yiddish as their national tongue. Indonesia, the nation created by the struggle of thousands of islands against the Dutch colonial empire, also created its own language to have a medium of universal communication.

Gandhi, as we observed, was deeply troubled by the absence in India of a common language. He was ashamed that his immersion in English had made him neglect his native Gujarati. Even though English was already spoken by the Indian elites, Gandhi did not want the English he wrote so well to become the national language. He regarded English as the bearer of westernization. Indians, Gandhi decided, must learn to speak several Indian tongues. He held that in Europe nationalist movements were associated with the recovery of a formerly neglected language. His Jewish friends in South Africa had told him of the literary renaissance of Yiddish, previously a jargon without literature, despised by educated people.[13] He mentioned similar revivals among the Afrikaans. He claimed that Lloyd George, the English states-man of Welsh origin, wanted Welsh children to learn Welsh. He might also have mentioned Czech, Flemish, Finnish, and several other European languages that political domination had marginalized, were no longer spoken by the educated classes, had been reduced to a popular jargon, but were now, thanks to a nationalist revival, being recovered and cele-brated. Gandhi favoured a development of the Indian lan-guages so that the people in their own regions would be able to discuss all aspects of their social life in their own tongue. Gandhi realized how vulnerable languages are, including one's mother tongue. In situations where the public language is different, inherited languages quickly deteriorate, assume a folkloric character, are used only when speaking of family matters, and no longer suffice for dealing with all aspects of society, including science and politics. Gandhi knew some-thing of this humiliation.

Grand'Maison's ethics of nationalism includes concern for language. When the Parti Québécois, which Grand'Maison supported in his work of 1970, was elected as the provincial government in 1976, the new government declared French as the province's official language, even while continuing to support the historic anglophone institutions, such as schools, universities, hospitals, and social services. Since francophone Quebecers, a majority of eighty per cent in their province, constitute a small minority on the North American continent with its traditional English-only culture, these francophones believe – and I agree with them – that unless their language is protected by law, it will be replaced by English in the public sphere, reduced to a popular dialect, and eventually disappear altogether. Some English-speaking Quebecers appreciate this situation and for this reason gladly carry on their public life in French. They are proud of the survival of an alternative national culture in North America. Yet other English-speaking Quebecers regret the days of the past when the language used in commerce and industry was English, in Quebec the language of the minority. These English-speaking Quebecers have a negative opinion of Quebec nationalism. They find it insulting that a majority of eighty per cent demands that their language be the official tongue and used in public life, including public signs. Since English has become the world language, promoted by the technology of industrial production and electronic communication, the survival of French as Quebec's public language is, in my opinion, by no means certain, despite the protection of the law.

The multi-lingual nature of humanity confirms the Durkheimian argument that people are constituted by their integration into a national or cultural community. Implicit in undifferentiated universalism is the dream of humanity communicating in a single tongue. Esperanto was a liberal invention that did not recognize its own imperialist design: this artificial language was fashioned out of Western languages without the slightest relation to the languages of Asia and Africa. Looked upon from the global perspective, nationalism protects pluralism: nations stand against empire.

SOCIAL COHESION AS REACTION
TO GLOBALIZATION

Let me return to the new phenomenon of globalization to which I have already referred on a previous page.[14] Globalization is a complex historical process made possible through new technologies of communication and transportation. This process includes, in addition to universal free trade and the transnational nature of economic power, a new political interdependence, partly symbolized by the United Nations, new intercultural encounters at universities, interreligious institutes, and many other forums; a common reliance on the same scientific methodologies and the same technological development; and the creation of a consumer-oriented mono-culture uniting the elites in all parts of the world and exerting a strong appeal to the people everywhere. It is possible, as I have mentioned, to take a purely negative view of globalization. This is done by critics who focus exclusively on the globalization of unregulated capitalism, the power of the transnational corporations, and the marginalization of people, massively in the south and increasingly also in the north, who are no longer deemed economically useful either as workers or as consumers. But since globalization is more than universal free trade and includes political interdependence and inter-cultural exchange, it is wise to listen also to the more positive interpretations of this phenomenon.

The work of Roland Robertson on the spread of globalization reveals that the social conditions produced by it lay the foundation for a postmodern cuture.[15] New interrelations and new dependencies have destabilized traditional institutions, including the nation-state, and invalidated the corresponding traditional theories, making room for new forms of human association and new theories for interpreting social existence. "State-based societies become heavily porous. Globalization carries with it an implication for locality: the global and the local become part of the same dialectic. We enter a world not of standardization and homogenisation, but of difference and unpredictability."[16]

There are also economic reasons behind the recent turn to localism. Since national governments are increasingly unwilling or unable to protect the material well-being of their people, political leaders and activists in the regions try to mobilize the people to strengthen the regional economy. Since Washington and Ottawa do not intervene to halt de-industrialization and overcome unemployment, many governors of American states and premiers of Canadian provinces have assumed powers of independent action unprecedented in the past. In this context, Quebec is not so singular. But "state-based societies become heavily porous" also for cultural and ethnic reasons. In the new circumstance, communities and nations that were threatened by assimilation and prevented from self-development discover a new creativity – for instance the First Nations and Mexican Americans. Ethnicity assumes a new importance. Social scientists do not pretend to know where these developments will lead.

The above quotation of state-based societies becoming heavily porous is taken from an essay of a Scottish sociologist who interprets the emergence of a new Scottish nationalism. I introduced this topic in the first chapter.[17] Scottish nationalism stresses community against global individualism, social democracy against the dominant neo-conservatism, and self-determination against the central power of the Westminster government. To overcome poverty and unemployment the Scots must rely on their own inventiveness. The Christian literature that looks favourably on Scottish nationalism interprets it as a postmodern phenomenon.[18] In modern times, it is being argued, the small nation of Scotland was firmly embedded in a unitary state; it was overlooked by social scientists and political observers, and it was reluctant to celebrate its own history and emphasize its cultural difference. Yet at this postmodern moment, nationalists in Scotland affirm its identity as a nation, demand some form of self-government, look for a closer relationship of Scotland with the European Union, and show greater concern for poverty in the third world. This appears postmodern because it combines the local and the global in a new dynamic.

This takes us to the question of whether the economic, social, and political conditions of the present are initiating a new period of human history that can no longer be interpreted with the help of concepts useful for the understanding of the previous period, the age of modernity. If contemporary nationalism is a phenomenon related to globalization, it would have to be interpreted in categories that relate the local and the global in a new way. This debate has already begun among some social scientists. This topic lies beyond the scope of this book. Yet since the Christian literature reflecting favourably upon Scottish nationalism frequently refers to this topic, I wish to mention three points raised in this context.

First, since the utilitarianism spread by the global mono-culture creates an emptiness and spiritual homelessness among many people, they eagerly turn to a local or regional community that mediates a cultural heritage and offers them a set of shared values. In the words of Anthony Gidden:

In the conditions of day-to-day life in which routinisation has largely replaced tradition, and where "meaning" has retreated to the margins of the private and the public, feelings of communality of language and "belongingness" in a national community tend to form one strand contributing to the maintenance of ontological security.[19]

The second point made in this literature is that the new movements of identity politics do not intend to create sovereign states as independent entities but rather envisage new institutional arrangements for regulating power in the interaction between nations and the global community. They seek political self-determination in the context of shared responsibility.

Globalization has the effect of contrasting and dislocating the centred and "closed" identities of national cultures. It has a pluralising impact on these identities, producing a variety of new positions of identification and making these more political, more plural and diverse; less fixed, unified or transhistorical.[20]

The Scottish nationalism for which the Christian community has sympathy does not aim at national sovereignty. It recognizes the ambiguity of the autonomous nation-state. Its aim is rather the creation of structures, such as the return of the Scottish parliament to Edinburgh, that would make possible national self-determination in the context of new relationships with England and the countries of Europe.

The same Christian literature is, thirdly, concerned with the role of the Church of Scotland in the process of national reconstruction. Since the Church now represents only a minority of Scots, it can no longer speak for the whole nation. The Church must learn to act ecumenically. It must cooperate with Catholics and other Protestants who love social justice and care for their community. Since Christians have become marginal in Scottish society, they now know the frustration caused by being excluded from the dominant discourse. A marginal church, this literature proposes, should stand with other marginalized groups in society in support of social justice and pluralism.

Are these church people spelling out an impossible dream for the Scottish nation and Scottish church? Is globalization an earth-shaking event that will provoke the reorganization of society in new patterns of local-global relations? Or should we follow a pessimistic interpretation of present-day globalization and lament the destruction of human communities and the exclusion of peoples through the spread of the self-regulating market system and the unrestrained power of international capital?

Afterword

Philip Cercone, the editor-in-chief of McGill-Queen's University Press, has asked me to write an afterword to articulate my own evaluation of Quebec nationalism and offer my opinion on the political debate regarding the future of Quebec and Canada.

For twenty-eight years I taught theology and sociology at St Michael's College in the University of Toronto. During that time, I – an immigrant – became increasingly concerned with the public issues debated in Canada, and their ethical and theological implications. I studied the history of Canada and its political culture, involved myself in debates on matters of human rights and social justice, and became a member of the New Democratic Party and the Canadian Civil Liberties Association. In 1977, I was invited to teach one semester at the Religious Studies Faculty of McGill University; in 1981, I taught two semesters at the Département des sciences religieuses of UQAM (Université du Québec à Montréal); and in 1986, I moved permanently to Montreal to become a professor at McGill University's Religious Studies Faculty.

My move to Quebec was a great adventure. It was an entry into a different world. It almost felt like coming to a new country. I had the feeling that I was welcomed with open arms by the French-speaking society. The Jesuit community invited me to become a member of the editorial committee of their review, *Relations,* a monthly dealing with social and political issues from the perspective of faith and justice. In the past, *Relations* had been politically and ecclesiastically conservative, but from the seventies on, the review adopted a social democratic perspective and saw itself as a representative of the Catholic Left in Quebec. Through *Relations* I became involved in the important debates in Quebec society and active in a number of organizations, among them la Ligue des droits et libertés. While my life and work at McGill went on in English, my life in the wider community was increasingly carried on in French, a challenge for me that I thoroughly enjoyed. My experience, I may add, was not typical: many professors at McGill University work only in English and have little or no contact with the francophone society. Few are the intellectuals in Quebec who regularly cross the linguistic divide.

Relations regarded itself as a nationalist monthly, and most of my francophone friends were nationalists, whether they voted for the Parti Québécois (PQ) or the Liberal Party of Quebec (PLQ). For this reason I felt impelled to study the complex phenomenon of nationalism and nationalist movements. What concerned me in particular, as I mentioned in the first chapter of this book, was the ethical issue. Are there norms that allow one to distinguish between forms of nationalism that are ethically acceptable and forms that are ethically unacceptable? I was greatly impressed by the ethical norms formulated by the Catholic bishops of Quebec. According to them, as I have related, a political movement for national self-determination is ethical only if it intends to create a more just and more open society, promises to protect the rights of minorities, seeks cooperation with the adjacent nations, and refuses to make the nation the highest good. In other words, a nationalist movement must be evaluated by critically examining the social project it promotes. What kind of society does it want to create? My conclusion was that the mainstream of Quebec nationalism in the PQ and the PLQ lived up to the norms formulated by the bishops.

I was, of course, no stranger to nationalism. Since I was born in Germany, I had an experience of an ugly form of nationalism, carried by an intention to build a vast empire, subjugate other nations, and extirpate the Jews of Europe. Yet when living in Toronto, I supported what we then called "Canadian nationalism," promoted by the policies of the NDP, the Committee for an Independent Canada, and other political and cultural efforts intended to enhance Canadian autonomy and Canadian identity, and protecting them from being overwhelmed by American power and influence. As I said earlier, my friend Douglas Hall, the well-known Protestant theologian, has called this "nationalism at the edge of empire." While Canadian nationalism seems to be largely carried by an elite, Quebec nationalism, as I discovered when I moved to Montreal, is a people's movement. Quebec nationalism is deeply rooted in the experience of a people, conscious that its almost universally shared sense of identity does not fit the space assigned to Quebec in the Canadian federation.

*

This present form of Quebec nationalism is a fairly recent development. In the past, Quebec saw itself as the cradle and centre of the French-Canadian nation distributed over the whole of Canada. This was the position defended by Pierre Trudeau and, after him, by Jean Chrétien and Stéphane Dion. Yet in the Quiet Revolution of the early sixties, French-Canadians in Quebec (over eighty per cent of its population) expressed their political will to be "*maîtres chez nous*," masters in their own house, responsible for the orientation and development of their own society. They recognized that for most French-Canadians outside of Quebec, French remains the language cherished at home, while English has become the language they use when discussing public issues, professional matters, and scientific questions. If French is to survive in North America as a public discourse, it will only be in Quebec where it has majority status and can be protected by government legislation.

French Quebecers thus see themselves as a people, heirs of a long history, located within a given territory, responsible for their society, possessing a government, and attempting to create their own approach to economic development. They were greatly encouraged by the 1966 Covenant of the United Nations which recognized the human right of a people to political, cultural, and economic self-determination. In Quebec this claim transcended party affiliation. The federalist PLQ and, after its foundation, the sovereignist PQ were in agreement that Quebecers constituted a nation within Canada and had a right to political self-determination. They called the provincial legislature "*l'assemblée nationale*," the provincial highway "*la route nationale*," and Quebec City, the seat of the legislature, "*la capitale nationale*."

The old "ethnic nationalism" designed to defend the rights of French-Canadians in all parts of Canada has here been transformed into a "territorial nationalism," embracing all citizens of Quebec, whatever their ethnic origin. This was a painful experience for many French-Canadians outside of Quebec who have the same ethnic roots, but who are now no longer part of the family. The new definition of the Quebec people, adopted by the major public institutions in Quebec, the government, the political parties, the Catholic Church, and other social institutions, now includes, besides the majority – the descendants of the early French settlers – the British community established since the end of the eighteenth century as well as the communities created by immigrants and their descendants. The territorial definition of the Quebec people has remained open to the self-definition of the Native peoples.

The official self-understanding of Quebec has become pluralistic. French Quebecers see themselves as a people with cultural roots going back three centuries, capable of receiving communities of other origins and embracing them as citizens on an equal footing. This change found solemn expression in the Quebec Charter of Rights, published in 1975, five years prior to the Canadian Charter. While the Canadian Charter dealt only with political rights, it is not insignificant that the Quebec Charter, following the Universal Declaration of Human Rights of 1948, also includes people's socio-economic rights, such as the right to work, food, shelter, clothing, education, and health care. This difference reveals the social democratic orientation of the new Quebec created by the Quiet Revolution.

Since I studied Quebec nationalism from an ethical perspective, I paid special attention to the new pluralism. According to Paul Tillich's ethico-political reflections examined in chapter 4 of this book, it is a mistake to think that to create greater justice in society, people must give up the attachment to their historical origin. The "myth of origin," as Tillich called it, must not be forgotten, but opened up and rethought in the light of justice – the "myth of demand." If this is correct, then doing justice to the new pluralism does not interrupt but rather enriches and expands cultural continuity in Canada and Quebec.

There were good reasons, then, why the Quebec government under the Liberals and the PQ, while recognizing Quebec's pluri-ethnic character, refused to accept the multicultural policy of the federal government. According to the federal definition of multiculturalism, Canada is a bilingual country possessing a plurality of cultures, none of which enjoys a privileged position. But is this a coherent position? If there are two official languages, then schools and universities will teach in one of these languages, introduce students to the literature of this one language, and study the history of how this language arrived in Canada. An officially bilingual country, therefore, inevitably privileges the cultures that correspond to the official languages. What is demanded by justice is that the two historical cultures welcome the arriving cultures and start interacting with them. It is worth mentioning that Canada's political culture, including that of Quebec, is of British origin – and is being rapidly adopted by immigrant communities of whatever cultural background. Only the First Nations want to be faithful to their own institutions of self-organization.

Quebec has defined its cultural pluralism differently than the federal government. The Quebec government under the Liberals and the PQ has distinguished between the receiving culture of Quebec and the arriving cultures brought from other parts. To encourage the dynamic interaction between these cultures and strengthen the cohesion of society as a whole, different policies have been advocated over the years. At one time the emphasis has been on "the convergence of cultures," which supposes that the dynamic interaction of these cultures modifies both the receiving and the arriving cultures, bringing them closer together without eliminating the identity of the arriving cultures. Another effort to honour pluralism and create a cohesive society has been the search for "a common public culture," i.e. a set of values shared by all, enabling the citizens, whatever their cultural background, to work together for the common good – and, at the same time, allowing the cultural communities to remain distinct and to flourish. At present, the emphasis of the Quebec government is on "education for citizenship," or teaching people, whatever their ethnic origin, to make full use of the human rights guaranteed by the Quebec Charter and to involve themselves in the promotion of civil society. One reason why I follow these policies and practices with great attention is that I am an active member of a committee on intercultural relations, appointed by the Quebec bishops, the task of which it is to promote a better understanding of pluralism in Church and society.

Despite the public acknowledgment of pluralism, ethnocentrism and racism have not suddenly disappeared from society. As a member of the Canadian Civil Liberties Association I was keenly aware of this in English Canada, and now, as a member of la Ligue des droits et libertés, I am fully aware of this phenomenon in Quebec. The Quebec government has created a special body, le Conseil des droits de la personne, with the power to investigate and prosecute acts of ethnic discrimination. As in Toronto, people in Montreal committed to the struggle against racism are able to join a variety of social organizations that counsel persons experiencing discrimination, help refugees and immigrants, sustain women in their struggle for equality, support gays and lesbians in their effort to be publicly respected, and in general promote a culture of openness. Quebec is a democratic society with the potentialities and failures shared by other Western societies.

*

In the above observations I have made no distinction between federalists and sovereignists in Quebec. The difference between the PLQ and the PQ is not, in my opinion, a major one. Both parties oppose the federalism presently defended by Ottawa. Between "renewed federalism" recognizing the Quebec nation, demanded by the Liberals, and "sovereignty-association" envisaged by the PQ, there is not a great deal of difference. More than that, in my opinion, the efforts of Quebec to solve its problems – the protection of French as the public language and the promotion of social justice – will remain the same, whatever its political future. Let me explain what I mean by this.

Quebec is a unique island in North America, an anomaly, a society and a space, the public language of which is other than English. Unless the French tongue is protected by law, as it is presently in Quebec, it will gradually disappear from public life and become a folkloric language used in family and neighbourhood, as it is in Lousiana. As an immigrant I am very sensitive to the vulnerability of languages. Immigrants are well aware that unless they make a special effort, they do not keep their mother tongue intact: they begin to use words taken from the public language, employ grammatical constructions not acceptable in their mother tongue, and gradually lose their ability to speak correctly of public, professional, and scientific matters in their native language. On visits to their country of origin, they discover that because of their many mistakes, people there smile at them. English-speaking people, I have found, do not easily grasp the fragility of language.

What I infer from this linguistic vulnerability is that law alone will not protect the French language. To keep it alive and creative as the public medium of communication and the language of science and technology will always remain a cultural struggle, even if Quebec became a sovereign nation. At present, English is becoming the lingua franca of the globe: it is used almost universally in the industrial and financial world, in technology and the sciences, at international academic conferences and in the field of international politics. The globalization of neo-liberal capitalism is taking place in English. Almost three-quarters of worldwide research in the natural and social sciences is published in English. While it is a great advantage to have, for the first time in history, a language making possible universal communication, the advantage also has problematic aspects. At international conferences, people whose mother tongue is not English are forced to express themselves in a language not their own: hence they can say only what they are able to say, and not what they really wish to say. At the same time, English-speakers come to feel that they need not learn other languages to be in touch with global developments. In some parts of the world, countries are beginning to protect the status of their language in public life and the sciences against the increasing pressure of English.

In Quebec, this small francophone space in North America, the cultural weight of English is an overwhelming reality. It is no wonder that the majority of non-francophone immigrants in Quebec prefer integration into the English rather than the French-speaking community, English being the language of this continent. It is not surprising that many small and medium-sized businesses in Montreal want to keep English as the language of work. Even if large enterprises are obliged by law to operate in French, the trend is to keep as much English as possible. If you buy a car in Quebec, the dashboard speaks to you in English. It is possible to move to Quebec, become a professor at an anglophone university, live here for twenty or thirty years, and never learn to speak French. Despite the laws demanding French on public signs and its use as the language of work in large enterprises, English is omnipresent in science and technology, on the internet, and in the world of business and investment. Will Montreal remain officially French-speaking? Will French survive as the public language of Quebec society? Some English-speaking groups in Quebec, unhappy with the language legislation, invoke their personal human rights and try to shame the French-speaking majority for using the law to protect their linguistic and cultural identity. Yet the heavy linguistic pressure is not caused by the politics of a few anglophone groups: it is due, rather, to an objective reality, the cultural weight of the English language in North America. Whether Quebec remains part of Canada or becomes a sovereign nation will not change this linguistic situation: to keep French alive and creative, make it the language of commerce and industrial production, and keep it as the means of communication in science and technology will always demand a cultural struggle calling for personal commitment.

What about social justice in Quebec? Originally the PQ was committed to social democracy in keeping with the democratic socialist ideals associated with the Quiet Revolution. When the PQ wanted to join the Socialist International, the NDP, an active member of that association, prevented this, arguing that membership is open only to one party of a single country. Yet under the impact of free market globalization and the neo-liberal ideology legitimating it, the present PQ government has abandoned its social democratic orientation. Because it received the support of the labour movement and the popular sector, the government makes occasional gestures signifying that its aim is to create a participatory society, but these gestures do not affect the dominant orientation. In Quebec, as in all capitalist countries today, the gap between rich and poor is increasing and a growing sector of the population finds itself at the margin of society.

In Quebec, the response to this situation has been an outburst of social energy among the low-income sector – a movement paralleled today in all capitalist countries – promoting community social and economic development to transform the lives of tens of thousands of people. In Quebec, we speak of "le mouvement communautaire" and "l'économie sociale." Because Quebecers have always had to struggle to preserve their collective identity, they have a long tradition of cooperative activities. In the present situation, this tradition of solidarity is finding expression in a growing network of groups and associations involved in self-help projects and small-scale, democratically organized enterprises, revitalizing civil society from the bottom up. There may be some advantages in being a small group obliged to struggle for cultural survival: there are many European examples of small states (Belgium, Denmark, Austria) and small communities (the Basques, the Catalonians, the Scots) that reveal remarkable economic creativity.

While social and economic development at the grassroots cannot transform the whole of society, the movement at the base does create an alternative culture where work is embedded in community relations and where all have their say – at odds with the dominant system. The spread of a critical culture rooted in people's self-organization generates new ideas, attitudes, and practices that may eventually, under new conditions, affect society as a whole. A growing number of people in all societies, including Quebec, are withdrawing from engagement in party politics and supporting instead the community movements in their neighbourhood.

What I conclude from these brief reflections is that whether Quebec leaves or stays in the Canadian federation will have little effect on the struggle in that society for greater social justice. The federal government, the PQ, and the PLQ appear to stand for the same neo-liberal policies. Where I see social creativity and the emergence of new ideas and practices is in the movements at the base renewing civil society.

*

Even though I do not see much difference between the PQ and the PLQ, I must ask myself the question how I will vote. What I want is very clear: I desire a renegotiation of the Canadian federation that recognizes the nationhood of Quebec and the right to self-government of the Native peoples. This is what seems eminently just to me. But there is no likelihood that this will occur under the present conditions. Previous efforts in this direction have failed.

Why is it that English-speaking Canadians are so unwilling to recognize Quebec as a nation? The English in Great Britain have no hesitation in regarding the Scots as a nation, even though many people living in Scotland are not of Scottish origin and many Scots actually live in England, some belonging to the upper echelon. One difference is that the Scottish people have a history going back to the medieval times, while the history of Quebec is only three and half centuries old. There are still many Canadians, especially in Ontario, who have not forgotten that Confederation in 1867 was praised by many political leaders as a union between two peoples or, in the vocabulary of those days, between two races. Yet most Canadians, I think, especially in the western provinces, and also among the cultural communities of more recent origin, see Canada as an English-speaking country with a French-speaking minority concentrated in the province of Quebec. Most English-speaking Canadians, I believe, do not recognize that by defining Canada as a country of ten equal provinces, the Constitution of 1982 violated Quebec's self-understanding as a nation. That is why Quebec has not signed this document.

Since there exist many bi-national or pluri-national states in the world, it is not easy to fathom why Canada has been opposed to such an idea. I am unwilling to interpret this refusal as bad will or a desire to dominate. I prefer to think that the daily experience of English-speaking Canadians in most parts of the country convinces them that Canada is a English-speaking, pluri-ethnic society, in which several ethnic communities try to preserve their language, culture, and identity. Unless one has had a personal experience of the integral distinctiveness of Quebec and personally witnessed the spontaneous self-understanding of Quebecers as constituting their own society, it is almost impossible for Canadians in the rest of the country to understand what the recognition of nationhood mean to Quebecers. To have such a personal experience it is, needless to say, necessary to understand and to speak French. Since English has become such a global language, first through the British empire and later through US-based science, technology, and consumer culture, people whose mother tongue is English know that they will be understood in the cities of the world and hence find it more difficult to learn other languages. English-speaking North America is perhaps the only region in the world where educated people, including academics, are, for the most part, able to speak only one language. This, I think, adds to the difficulty of appreciating Quebec's historical identity.

It is to me equally sad that the citizens of Canada and Quebec, for the most part, lack the awareness that our own collective history has reduced the Native peoples to their present humiliated state and that we owe them, late though it be, recognition and restitution.

Since I believe that the recognition of Quebecers as a nation is part of justice, I think that English-speaking Canada, supported by the present policy of the federal government, is pushing Quebecers in a direction they do not want to go. What they want is the recognition of their national identity and the corresponding powers – either in the form of special status as proposed by the PLQ or in the form of sovereignty-association as advocated by the PQ. Yet Canada seems unwilling to acknowledge this. In the early sixties, the three federal political parties, Liberal, Conservative, and New Democratic, envisaged such an unequal federalism. Yet this openness was replaced by the political perspective of Pierre Elliot Trudeau who persuaded English-speaking Canadians that their country was made up of ten equal provinces. Prior to the 1980 referendum, in his speech at Montreal's Paul Sauvé Arena in support of the vote against sovereignty, Trudeau promised his audience that he would see to it that their No would not be interpreted by the rest of Canada as an expression of their satisfaction with the status quo. Yet, against his promise, he pushed through a repatriation of the Constitution that Quebec was unwilling to accept and advocated a formula of change that is likely to prevent Quebec from becoming a recognized nation or distinctive society in Canada. Nor does the Canadian Confederation respect the national identities of the aboriginal people. With political scientists such as Kenneth McRoberts, Philip Resnick, James Tully, and Jeremy Webber, I regard the rigid understanding of the Canadian Confederation, unresponsive to the national claims within it, as a transgression against democracy. In my opinion Quebec will be heard only if it speaks from a position of strength. It is ironic that Quebecers, like myself, who are deeply attached to Canada and desire a more just Canadian Confederation, will have to vote Yes at the next referendum. If there is another way to justice, I am ready to hear it.

Notes

CHAPTER ONE

1 "United Nations International Covenant on Civil and Political Rights" in Walter Laqueur, ed., *The Human Rights Reader* (New York: New American Library, 1990), 215–24.

2 Mark A. Noll, *Christians in the American Revolution* (Grand Rapids, MI: Christian University Press, 1977).

3 Cf. Pierre Chariton, *Le droit des peuples à leur identité: L'évolution d'une question dans l'histoire du christianisme* (Montreal: Fides, 1979).

4 Judith Dwyer, ed., *The New Dictionary of Catholic Social Thought* (Collegeville, MN: Liturgical Press, 1994).

5 Margerie Villier, *Charles Péguy* (London: Collins, 1965), 374.

6 See Jim Forest, "A Dialogue on Reconciliation in Belgrade" in Gregory Baum and Harold Wells, eds, *The Reconciliation of Peoples* (Maryknoll, NY: Orbis Books, 1997), 110–17.

7 "Le peuple québécois et son avenir politique" (15 August 1979) and "Construire ensemble une société meilleure"(9 January 1980). See Gérard Rochais, ed., *La justice comme bonne nouvelle: Messages sociaux, économiques et politiques des évêques du Québec* (Montreal: Bellarmin, 1984), 137–56.

8 For an analysis, see Gregory Baum, "The Bishops and Quebec Nationalism," in his *The Church in Quebec* (Montreal: Novalis, 1991), 159–70. Also see David Seljak's doctoral dissertation, "The Catholic Church's Reaction to the Secularization of Nationalism in Quebec," Faculty of Religious Studies, McGill University, 1995.

9 See Gregory Baum, *The Church for Others: Protestant Theology in Communist East Germany* (Grand Rapids, MI: Eerdmans, 1996).

10 For the encyclical *Sollicitudo rei socialis* and commentaries, see Gregory Baum and Robert Ellsberg, eds., *The Logic of Solidarity* (Maryknoll, NY: Orbis Books, 1989). The reformability of communism and capitalism is the encyclical's main point. See my commentary, pp 85–7.

11 See William Storrar, *Scottish Identity and Christian Vision* (Edinburgh: The Handsel Press, 1990); *Christianity and Social Vision*, Occasional Paper No. 20, 1990, and *Seeing Scotland, Seeing Christ*, Occasional Paper No. 28, 1993, Centre for Theology and Public Issues, Edinburgh.

12 See, for instance, Benedict Anderson, *Imagined Communities: Reflections on the Origin and Spread of Nationalism* (Thetford, Norfolk: Verso, 1983); Ernest Gellner, *Nations and Nationalism* (Oxford: Blackwell, 1983); Eric Hobsbawm, *Nations and Nationalism Since 1870: Programme, Myth, Reality* (Cambridge: Cambridge University Press, 1990); Anthony Smith, *Nationalism in the Twentieth Century* (New York: New York University Press, 1978).

13 George Grant, *Lament for a Nation* (Toronto: McClelland & Stewart, 1965).

14 See the article on Nationalism in *The Canadian Encyclopedia*, 1985 edition, 2:1199–200. Also see William Christian and Colin Campbell, *Political Parties and Ideologies in Canada* (Toronto: McGraw Hill Ryerson, 1974).

15 Kari Levitt, *Silent Surrender* (Toronto: Macmillan, 1970).

16 See the article on Committee for an Independent Canada in *The Canadian Encyclopedia*, 1985 edition, 1:379.

17 See Douglas Hall, *The Canada Crisis* (Toronto: Anglican Book Centre, 1980), 41.

18 Kari Levitt in Kenneth McRobbie, ed., *Humanity, Society and Commitment: On Karl Polanyi* (Montreal: Black Rose, 1994), 117.

CHAPTER TWO

1 Maurice Friedman, *Encounter on the Narrow Ridge: The Life of Martin Buber* (New York: Paragon House, 1991); Laurence Silberstein, *Martin Buber's Social and Religious Thought* (New York: New York University Press, 1989); Bernard Susser, *Existence and Utopia: the Social and Political Thought of Martin Buber* (Rutherford: Fairleigh Dickenson University Press, 1981).

2 In English translation, *Community and Society* (New York: Harper Torchbook, 1963).

3 On Weber's critique of instrumental rationality, see Robert Nisbet, *The Sociological Tradition* (New York: Basic Books, 1966), 292–300.

4 The Weberian critique of modernity has been further developed by the Protestant theologian Jacques Ellul (see *The Technological Society*, New York: Vintage Press, 1964) and by two sociologists who occasionally write on theological themes, Peter Berger (see *The Homeless Mind*, New York: Random House, 1973) and David Lyon (see *The Information Society*, Cambridge: Polity, 1988).

5 Quoted in Silberstein, *Martin Buber's Social and Religious Thought*, 38.

6 For the English translation of the three speeches, see N.N. Glatzer, ed., *Martin Buber: On Judaism* (New York: Schocken Books, 1967).

7 Ibid., 16.

8 Ibid., 17.

9   Ibid., 15.

10 Ibid., 18.

11 Friedman, *Encounter on the Narrow Ridge*, 58.

12 Glatzer, *Martin Buber: On Judaism*, 20.

13 Ibid., 38.

14 Ibid., 111.

15 Ibid., 111–12.

16 Quoted in Silberstein, *Martin Buber's Social and Religious Thought*, 67.

17 See my remarks on Charles Péguy and French Catholic nationalism, 7.

18 Quoted in Wulf Kopke, *Lion Feuchtwanger* (Munic: Verlag Textkritik, 1983), 55.

19 For Émile Durkheim's argument of community as matrix of personal existence, see Robert Nisbet, *Emile Durkheim* (Englewood, NJ: Prentice-Hall, 1965).

20 Susser, *Existence and Utopia*, 138.

21 An English translation of Buber's speech on nationalism given at the 1921 Zionist Congress was published in the collection of essays, *Israel and the Word*, by Martin Buber, 214–26 (New York: Schocken Books, 1948). This quotation is from p. 215.

22 Ibid., 216.

23 Ibid., 221.

24 Ibid., 224.

25 "The Land and Its Possessors – From an Open Letter to Gandhi." Ibid., 227–33.

26 "The Gods of the Nations and God," Ibid., 197–213, 202.

27 In his book *Paths into Utopia* (New York: Macmillan, 1950), Buber develops his idea of a moral, cooperative socialism, at odds with Marxist socialism and in fact repudiated by it.

28 Paul R. Mendes-Flohr, ed., *A Land of Two Peoples: Martin Buber on Jews and Arabs* (New York: Oxford University Press, 1983), 194.

29 Ibid., 217.

CHAPTER THREE

1 W.M. Theodore de Bary, ed., *Sources of Indian Tradition*, Vol. II (New York: Columbia University Press, 1968), 108. The original texts and the historical commentaries contained in this collection are my main source in the present chapter. Since *Sources of Indian Tradition* contains only the main sections of Gandhi's pamphlet *Hind Swaraj*, I shall occasionally cite this work from *The Collected Works of Mahatma Gandhi*, Vol. x, Government of India, Ministry of Information and Broadcasting, The Publication Division, 1963.

2 For historical accounts of the Moderates and the Extremists, see *Sources of Indian Tradition*, 108–52 and 153–86 respectively.

3 Gandhi reaffirmed the position he took in *Hind Swaraj* in 1938 and again in 1945. See *Sources of Indian Tradition*, 251, and Peter Brock, *The Mahatma and Mother India, Essays on Gandhi's Non-Violence and Nationalism* (Ahmedabad, India: Navajivan Publishing, 1983), 99.

4 See chapter 2.

5 *Sources of Indian Tradition*, 253.

6 M.A. Buch, *Rise and Growth of Indian Nationalism* (Baroda, India: Baroda College Press), 67.

7 *Sources of Indian Tradition*, 254.

8 Ibid., 255.

9 Ibid., 255.

10 Ibid., 259.

11 Ibid., 256.

12 Ibid., 258.

13 Ibid., 259.

14 Ibid., 262.

15 Ibid., 263.

16 Ibid., 267.

17 The best known scholar and activist is Vandana Shiva, founder of the Indian Research Foundation of Science, Technology and

Natural Resource Policy and author of *Ecology and the Politics of Survival: Conflicts over Natural Resources in India* (Tokyo and New Delhi: United Nations University Press and Sage Publication, 1991), and *The Violence of the Green Revolution* (London and Penang, Malaysia: Zed Books and Third World Network, 1991).

18 Brock, *The Mahatma and Mother India*, 91.

19 *Collected Works*, Vol. x, 27.

20 Brock, *The Mahatma and Mother India*, 93–4.

21 Max Müller, *India: What Can it Teach us?* (1883) and Henry Sumner Maine, *Village Communities in the East and West* (1871).

22 Brock, *The Mahatma and Mother India*, 95.

23 Ibid., 97.

24 *Collected Works*, Vol. x, 28–32.

25 *Sources of Indian Tradition*, 237. For a detailed study, see Sheila MacDonough, *Gandhi's Responses to Islam* (New Delhi, India: D.K. Printworld, 1994).

26 Brock, *The Mahatma and Mother India*, 105–6.

27 *Collected Works*, Vol. x, 57.

28 Erik Erikson, *Gandhi's Truth* (New York: Norton, 1969), 259, quoted by Brock, 109.

29 Brock, *The Mahatma and Mother India*, 106, 107.

30 For the documentation of the debate between Tagore and Gandhi, see *Sources of Indian Tradition*, 236–70.

31 Most famous is Alexis de Tocqueville's analysis in his *Democracy in America* (1840), which recognized the unprecedented power enjoyed by the modern state and described the state's temptation, in the name of reason and the public good, to exercise total control and become an instrument of domination. *Democracy in America*, Vol. ii (New York: Random House, 1945), 321–39.

32 *Sources of Indian Tradition*, 231.

33 Ibid., 239.

34 Tagore was reconciled to Gandhi in 1933 during Gandhi's first fast against untouchability. Ibid., 231.

35 Ibid., 242.

36 Ibid., 268.

37 Ibid., 269.

38 Ibid.

39 Brock, *The Mahatma and Mother India*, 98.

40 *Sources of Indian Tradition*, 270.

41 For this and the following two quotations, see R.R. Kasliwal, "Gandhi's Notion of the State," in D.K. Misca, ed., *Gandhi and Social Order*, (Delhi: Research Publication in Social Science, no date), 31.

CHAPTER FOUR

1 Tillich published *Blätter für religiösen Sozialismus*, 1920–27, and *Neue Blätter für den Sozialismus*, 1928–32.

2 *The Socialist Decision*, the English translation of Tillich's *Die sozialistische Entscheidung*, was published only in 1977 (New York: Harper & Row) with an excellent introduction by John R. Stumme. The original German text can be found in volume II of Tillich's *Gesammelte Werke* (Stuttgart: Evangelisches Verlagswerk, 1962) which also contains other essays of his on religious socialism.

3 Tillich, *The Socialist Decision*, xxxi.

4 See Gregory Baum, *Karl Polanyi on Ethics and Economics* (Montreal: McGill-Queen's University Press, 1996), 50.

5 H. Richard Niebuhr, *The Meaning of Revelation* (New York: Macmillan, 1960), 115.

6 See pages 31, 37 above. Also Maurice Friedman, *Encounter on the Narrow Ridge: The Life of Martin Buber* (New York: Paragon House, 1991), 55–72.

7 Ernst Bloch, *Geist der Utopie*, published in 1918, and Karl Mannheim, *Ideologie und Utopia*, published in 1928.

8 See Karl Polanyi, *The Great Transformation* (Boston: Beacon Press, 1957), and Gregory Baum, *Karl Polanyi on Ethics and Economics* (Montreal: McGill-Queen's University Press, 1996).

9 See Georg Lukacs, *Geschichte und Klassenbewusstsein* (1923). When Tillich was a professor at the University of Frankfurt, he was the director of Adorno's dissertation and promoted Horkheimer's appointment as professor. For the critique of Enlightenment modernity of these two thinkers, written during World War II, see T.W. Adorno and M. Horkheimer, *Dialectic of Enlightenment* (New York: Seabury Press, 1972).

10 James Reimer, *The Emanuel Hirsch and Paul Tillich Debate* (Lewiston, NY: E. Mellen Press, 1989).

11 Harold Wells, *A Future for Socialism?: Political Theology and "the Triumph of Capitalism"* (Valley Forge, PA: Trinity Press International, 1996).

CHAPTER FIVE

1 Jacques Grand'Maison, *Nationalisme et religion*, 2 vols. (Montréal: Beauchemin, 1970).

2 This and the following quotation are cited in William Kilbourne, *The Making of Canada* (Toronto: The Canadian Centennial Publishing Company, 1965), 12–13.

3 See my remarks on Canadian nationalism on pages 14–16.

4 Douglas Hall, "A View from the Edge of Empire," *ARC* (McGill University) 19 (1992), 21–33.

5 See the article on Jura (canton) in *The New Encyclopedia Britannica* (Chicago, 1992), 6:659.

6 *Cf.* Ninian Smart, "Religion, Myth and Nationalism," in Peter Merkl and Ninian Smart, eds., *Religion and Politics in the Modern World* (New York: New York University, 1983), 15–28. Also David Seljak, "Is Nationalism a Religion: A Critique of Ninian Smart," *ARC* (McGill University) 19 (1992): 33–45.

7 United Nations International Covenant on Civil and Political Rights (1966), Article 1, 1. See Walter Laqueur, ed., *The Human Rights Reader* (New York: New American Library, 1979), 215.

8 Grand'Maison, *Nationalisme et religion*, 1:47.

9 Ibid., 2:180.

10 See above p. 30.

11 This theme has been taken by Charles Taylor in several of his works. For a recent treatment, see Charles Taylor, "Why do Nations have to Become States," in *Reconciling the Solitudes: Essays on Canadian Federalism and Nationalism* (Montreal: McGill-Queen's University Press, 1993), 40–58.

12 Grand'Maison, *Nationalisme et religion*, 2:40 (my translation).

13 Ibid., 2:39 (my translation).

14 See the article "Corporatism" in Judith Dwyer, ed., *The New Dictionary of Catholic Social Teaching* (Collegeville, MN: Liturgical Press, 1994), 244–6.

15 Grand'Maison, *Nationalisme et religion*, 1:18 (my translation).

16 See Gregory Baum, *Catholics and Canadian Socialism* (Toronto: Lorimer, 1980), 183–5.

17 Grand'Maison, *Nationalisme et religion*, 2:19.

18 As an excellent book, among many titles, I recommend Kenneth McRoberts *Quebec: Social Change and Political Crisis* (Toronto: McClelland & Stewart, 3rd edition, 1988).

19 See Gregory Baum, *The Church in Quebec* (Montreal: Novalis, 1991), 15–47.

20 Jacques Grand'Maison, *La nouvelle classe et l'avenir du Québec* (Montréal: Éditions Alain Stanké, 1979).

21 Grand'Maison, *Nationalisme et religion*, 2:183–4 (my translation).

CHAPTER SIX

1 See pp 9–10 above.

2 I was told this several years ago by Rabbi Steven Schwarzschild of the Jewish Fellowship of Reconciliation.

3 Benedict Anderson, *Imagined Communities: Reflections on the Origin and Spread of Nationalism* (Thetford, Norfolk: Verso, 1983).

4 "We shall call 'ethnic groups' those human groups that entertain a subjective belief in their common descent because of similarities of exterior habitus or of custom or of both, or because of memories of colonization and migration; this belief must be important for the propagation of group formation." Max Weber in *Economy and Society*, G. Roth and C. Wittig, eds. (New York: Westminster, 1968), 389.

5 Ernest Gellner, *Nations and Nationalism* (Oxford: Blackwell, 1983); Eric Hobsbawm, *Nations and Nationalism Since 1870: Programme, Myth, Reality* (Cambridge: Cambridge University Press, 1990).

6 Jean-François Lyotard, *The Postmodern Condition* (Manchester: Manchester University Press, 1986). On the topic of postmodernism and the end of historical projects, see Gregory Baum, *Essays in Critical Theology* (Kansas City: Sheed and Ward, 1994), 77–95.

7 Michael Ignatieff, *Blood and Belonging* (Toronto: Viking, 1993).

8 See Gregory Baum, "Ethnic Pluralism in Quebec," *Canadian Forum*, April 1996, 19–22.

9 Gregory Baum, "The Role of the Churches in German-Polish Reconciliation," in Gregory Baum and Harold Wells, eds., *The Reconciliation of Peoples* (Maryknoll, NY: Orbis Books, 1997), 129–43.

10 Georg-Eckert-Institute für internationale Schulbuchforschung, Celler Str. 3, D-38114 Braunschweig.

11 *The Collected Works of Mahatma Gandhi*, Vol. x, Government of India, Ministry of Information and Broadcasting, The Publication Division, 1963, 41.

12 See *Quebec in a New World: The PQ's Plan for Sovereignty*, especially Duncan Cameron's foreword (Toronto: James Lorimer, 1994).

13 Peter Brock, *The Mahatma and Mother India* (Ahmedabad, India: Navajivan Publishing, 1983), 106.

14 See pp 16–17 above.

15 Roland Robertson, *Globalization: Social Theory and Global Culture* (London: Sage, 1992).

16 David McCrone, "Understanding Scotland: A Sociological Perspective," in *Seeing Scotland, Seeing Christ*, Occasional Paper No. 28, Centre for Theology and Public Issues, New College, Edinburgh, 1993, 3–13, 5.

17 See pp 11–13 above.

18 See William Storrar, *Scottish Identity and Christian Vision* (Edinburgh: The Handsel Press, 1990); *Christianity and Social Vision*, Occasional Paper No. 20, 1990, and *Seeing Scotland, Seeing Christ*, Occasional Paper No. 28, 1993, Centre for Theology and Public Issues, Edinburgh.

19 Quoted in *Seeing Scotland, Seeing Christ*, 11.

20 A quotation of Stuart Hall, cited in *Seeing Scotland, Seeing Christ*, 6.

Index

Index

Gandhi, Mahatma: the pamphlet *Hind Swaraj*, 42–7; India as a nation, 39–40, 50; ethical nationalism, 47–54; South African racism, 41–2; Hindu-Muslim solidarity, 51–2; nationalism serves universalism, 59–60; nationalism and language, 52–4; debate with Tagore, 54–60; opposition to modernity; 45–6, 48; non-violent Hinduism, 41, 46–7, 83; problematic nature of nation state, 60; the language of India, 130

Gellner, Ernest, 116

German-Polish reconciliation, 134

Giddens, Anthony, 134

Grand'Maison, Jacques: definitions of nation and nationalism, 85–8; ambiguity of the nation state, 88–90; neo-nationalism, 89–90; tension between particularism and universalism in the Bible, 90–3; antagonism between nation and empire, 94–5; Quebec nationalism prior to Quiet Revolution (1960), 95–101; the Church and Quebec nationalism, 96–7; messianic nationalism, 99–100; the nationalism of the Parti Québécois, 101–5; a statement on nationalism by Quebec theologians, 105–7, protection of the French language, 130–1

Grant, George, 15–16

Groulx, Lionel, 97–100

Haam, Ahad, 26–7

Habermas, Jürgen, 118

Hall, Douglas, 16, 87, 139

Herzl, Theodor, 26

Hirsch, Emanuel, 82

Hobsbawm, Eric, 116

Ignatieff, Michael, 120

Kant, Immanuel, 50

Keynes, John Maynard, 128

Kierkegaard, Søren, 28

Kohn, Hans, 28

Lévesque, Georges-Henri, 100

Levitt, Kari, 15, 17

Lukacs, Georg, 20

Lyotard, Jean-François, 119

McRoberts, Kenneth, 150

Maine, Henry Sumner, 53

Marx, Marxism, 11, 20, 63, 76, 112–13, 120, 127

Müller, Max, 51